Communicating the Appraisal: The Uniform Residential Appraisal Report

Second Edition

by Arlen C. Mills, MAI, SRA
and
Dorothy Z. Mills, SRA

Appraisal Institute
875 N. Michigan Avenue
Chicago, IL 60611-1980

Acknowledgments

Vice President, Publications: Christopher Bettin
Manager, Book Development: Michael R. Milgrim, PhD
Editor: Stephanie Shea-Joyce
Graphic Designer: Claire Baldwin

For Educational Purposes Only

The opinions and statements set forth herein reflect the viewpoint of the Appraisal Institute at the time of publication but do not necessarily reflect the viewpoint of each individual member. While a great deal of care has been taken to provide accurate and current information, neither the Appraisal Institute nor its editors and staff assume responsibility for the accuracy of the data contained herein. Further, the general principles and conclusions presented in this text are subject to local, state and federal laws and regulations, court cases and any revisions of the same. This publication is sold for educational purposes with the understanding that the publisher is not engaged in rendering legal, accounting or any other professional service.

Nondiscrimination Policy

The Appraisal Institute advocates equal opportunity and nondiscrimination in the appraisal profession and conducts its activities without regard to race, color, sex, religion, national origin, or handicap status.

Printed in the U.S.A.
03 02 01 00 99   6 5 4 3 2

Library of Congress Cataloging-in-Publication Data

Mills, Arlen C.
    Communicating the appraisal: the uniform residential appraisal report/Arlen C. Mills and Dorothy Z. Mills.
        p.   cm.
    ISBN 0-922154-15-5
    1. Dwellings—Valuation. 2. Real property—Valuation. I. Mills, Dorothy Z.   II. Title.
HD1387.M55 1994   93-48498
333.33'82—dc20   CIP

Table of Contents

Foreword v

Preface vi

Introduction 1

The Appraisal Report Form and the Valuation Process 3

Page One of the URAR Form 9

    A. Subject Identification 9

    B. Neighborhood Description 17

    C. PUD Project Information 25

    D. Site Description 27

    E. Description of Improvements 33

    F. Comments 45

Page Two of the URAR Form 49

    G. Cost Approach 49

    H. Sales Comparison Analysis 55

    I. Income Approach 65

    J. Reconciliation 67

Attachments to the URAR Form 71

Conclusions 76

Appendix 77

Readers of this text may be interested in purchasing the following Appraisal Institute products:

Texts
- *Communicating the Appraisal: The Narrative Report*

- *Communicating the Appraisal: The Small Residential Income Property Appraisal Report*

- *Communicating the Appraisal: The Individual Condominium or PUD Unit Appraisal Report*

- *The Appraisal of Real Estate*

- *The Dictionary of Real Estate Appraisal*

- *Appraising Residential Properties*

Videotape
- *The Small Residential Income Property Appraisal Report*

To order, contact:
Appraisal Institute
875 North Michigan Avenue
Chicago, IL 60611-1980
Attn: Order Fulfillment

Foreword

Residential appraisers have been using the Uniform Residential Appraisal Report form since it was introduced in 1986. In June 1993 a major revision to this essential form was announced and, to keep current, practitioners will need to become familiar with the new form and its required attachments.

This updated text in the *Communicating the Appraisal* series walks appraisers through the new URAR form, reviewing the sections that have remained unchanged and acquainting them with recent revisions. The changes to the form have been substantial. Its expanded comments sections and more flexible format encourage appraisers to provide detailed descriptions of all property components as well as thoughtful analysis of the factors that influence residential property values in the local market. Following the guidelines set forth in this book, appraisers can be confident that they understand the new form and are prepared to use it properly.

All appraisers know that the demands of their profession are high. Changes in the way appraisers do their work and report their findings provide new opportunities for growth. With the information in this guide, practitioners can continue to refine their craft and demonstrate their professionalism.

Douglas C. Brown, MAI
1994 President
Appraisal Institute

Preface

The increasing use of real estate appraisal report forms by government agencies, lending institutions, and other appraisal clients has made standardized forms and guidelines for their preparation a necessity. This publication provides appraisers with a detailed guide to the proper preparation of one such report, the Uniform Residential Appraisal Report (Freddie Mac Form 70/Fannie Mae Form 1004), also known as the URAR. An item-by-item analysis of the procedure for completing this widely used report form is presented along with pertinent references to the Uniform Standards of Professional Appraisal Practice and explanatory "appraisal notes" and "compliance notes."

The focus of this guidebook is the proper communication of a residential appraisal using the URAR form. Both experienced and novice residential appraisers will find it valuable in the performance of their daily assignments. The material in this guide is intended to augment educational programs and textbooks that teach residential valuation principles and methodology, not to replace them.

We would like to thank the many lenders and professional residential real estate appraisers who provided us with essential "field input" and insightful comments on the use of the new URAR, which was revised in June of 1993. We are also indebted to Mark Simpson, manager of Appraisal Standards for Fannie Mae, for his ongoing assistance and support. His valuable counsel has often been sought and is always appreciated.

Introduction

The Uniform Residential Appraisal Report (URAR) form, which is the subject of this guidebook in the *Communicating the Appraisal* series, was introduced in 1986 by the Federal National Mortgage Association (Fannie Mae) and the Federal Home Loan Mortgage Corporation (Freddie Mac). Representatives from the federal government and the nation's professional real estate appraisal organizations helped Fannie Mae and Freddie Mac guide the form through its development. Form appraisal reports were nothing new in 1986, but the release of the URAR was significant because it marked the first time that all major government agencies involved in mortgage activities agreed to employ the same report form. Since 1986 all mortgages issued by Fannie Mae, Freddie Mac, the Department of Housing and Urban Development, the Department of Veterans Affairs, and the Farmers Home Administration that may be sold in the secondary mortgage market must be based on appraisals presented on the URAR form.

In June 1993 a revised URAR was released. The new form is the result of a joint effort undertaken by government agencies and representative appraisal groups—including the Appraisal Institute and The Appraisal Foundation. The revisions represent improvements in the reporting of essential information and reflect changes in industry requirements and standards since the first version of the form was adopted.

The revised URAR has a two-page format with expanded space for comments. It may be used in its printed form or may be generated by software programs with expandability features to accommodate additional narrative. Either method of presentation is acceptable so long as the sales comparison analysis section, which appears on page two of the printed form, is presented on a single page, not over two or more pages.

When properly completed, the URAR form accompanied with the appropriate attachments can present a reliable picture of the valuation process, communicating the analysis of a single-family dwelling and the appraiser's value conclusions to both the users of residential appraisals and the purchasers of mortgages.

Figure 1 presents the two-page URAR form as revised in June 1993.

Figure 1. The URAR Form

UNIFORM RESIDENTIAL APPRAISAL REPORT — File No.

SUBJECT
Property Address — City — State — Zip Code
Legal Description — County
Assessor's Parcel No. — Tax Year — R.E. Taxes $ — Special Assessments $
Borrower — Current Owner — Occupant ☐ Owner ☐ Tenant ☐ Vacant
Property rights appraised ☐ Fee Simple ☐ Leasehold — Project Type ☐ PUD ☐ Condominium (HUD/VA only) HOA$ /Mo.
Neighborhood or Project Name — Map Reference — Census Tract
Sales Price $ — Date of Sale — Description and $ amount of loan charges/concessions to be paid by seller
Lender/Client — Address
Appraiser — Address

NEIGHBORHOOD
Location	☐ Urban	☐ Suburban	☐ Rural
Built up	☐ Over 75%	☐ 25-75%	☐ Under 25%
Growth rate	☐ Rapid	☐ Stable	☐ Slow
Property values	☐ Increasing	☐ Stable	☐ Declining
Demand/supply	☐ Shortage	☐ In balance	☐ Over supply
Marketing time	☐ Under 3 mos.	☐ 3-6 mos.	☐ Over 6 mos.

Predominant occupancy ☐ Owner ☐ Tenant ☐ Vacant (0-5%) ☐ Vacant (over 5%)
Single family housing PRICE $(000) AGE (yrs) — Low — High — Predominant
Present land use %: One family — 2-4 family — Multi-family — Commercial ( )
Land use change ☐ Not likely ☐ Likely ☐ In process To:

Note: Race and the racial composition of the neighborhood are not appraisal factors.
Neighborhood boundaries and characteristics:
Factors that affect the marketability of the properties in the neighborhood (proximity to employment and amenities, employment stability, appeal to market, etc.):
Market conditions in the subject neighborhood (including support for the above conclusions related to the trend of property values, demand/supply, and marketing time...such as data on competitive properties for sale in the neighborhood, description of the prevalence of sales and financing concessions, etc.):

PUD
Project information for PUDs (If applicable) — Is the developer/builder in control of the Home Owners' Association (HOA)? ☐ Yes ☐ No
Approximate total number of units in the subject project — Approximate total number of units for sale in the subject project
Describe common elements and recreational facilities:

SITE
Dimensions — Topography
Site area — Corner Lot ☐ Yes ☐ No — Size
Specific zoning classification and description — Shape
Zoning compliance ☐ Legal ☐ Legal nonconforming (Grandfathered use) ☐ Illegal ☐ No zoning — Drainage
Highest & best use as improved: ☐ Present use ☐ Other use (explain) — View
Landscaping / Driveway Surface / Apparent easements

Utilities	Public	Other	Off-site improvements	Type	Public	Private
Electricity	☐		Street		☐	☐
Gas	☐		Curb/gutter		☐	☐
Water	☐		Sidewalk		☐	☐
Sanitary sewer	☐		Street lights		☐	☐
Storm sewer	☐		Alley		☐	☐

FEMA Special Flood Hazard Area ☐ Yes ☐ No
FEMA Zone — Map Date
FEMA Map No.
Comments (apparent adverse easements, encroachments, special assessments, slide areas, illegal or nonconforming zoning use, etc.):

DESCRIPTION OF IMPROVEMENTS

GENERAL DESCRIPTION	EXTERIOR DESCRIPTION	FOUNDATION	BASEMENT	INSULATION
No. of Units	Foundation	Slab	Area Sq. Ft.	Roof ☐
No. of Stories	Exterior Walls	Crawl Space	% Finished	Ceiling ☐
Type (Det./Att.)	Roof Surface	Basement	Ceiling	Walls ☐
Design (Style)	Gutters & Dwnspts.	Sump Pump	Walls	Floor ☐
Existing/Proposed	Window Type	Dampness	Floor	None ☐
Age (Yrs.)	Storm/Screens	Settlement	Outside Entry	Unknown ☐
Effective Age (Yrs.)	Manufactured House	Infestation		

ROOMS	Foyer	Living	Dining	Kitchen	Den	Family Rm.	Rec. Rm.	Bedrooms	# Baths	Laundry	Other	Area Sq. Ft.
Basement												
Level 1												
Level 2												

Finished area above grade contains: Rooms; Bedroom(s); Bath(s); Square Feet of Gross Living Area

INTERIOR Materials/Condition	HEATING	KITCHEN EQUIP.	ATTIC	AMENITIES	CAR STORAGE
Floors	Type	Refrigerator ☐	None ☐	Fireplace(s) # ☐	None ☐
Walls	Fuel	Range/Oven ☐	Stairs ☐	Patio ☐	Garage # of cars
Trim/Finish	Condition	Disposal ☐	Drop Stair ☐	Deck ☐	Attached
Bath Floor	COOLING	Dishwasher ☐	Scuttle ☐	Porch ☐	Detached
Bath Wainscot	Central	Fan/Hood ☐	Floor ☐	Fence ☐	Built-In
Doors	Other	Microwave ☐	Heated ☐	Pool ☐	Carport
	Condition	Washer/Dryer ☐	Finished ☐		Driveway

Additional features (special energy efficient items, etc.):

COMMENTS
Condition of the improvements, depreciation (physical, functional, and external), repairs needed, quality of construction, remodeling/additions, etc.:
Adverse environmental conditions (such as, but not limited to, hazardous wastes, toxic substances, etc.) present in the improvements, on the site, or in the immediate vicinity of the subject property:

Freddie Mac Form 70 6-93 — PAGE 1 OF 2 — Fannie Mae Form 1004 6-93

Valuation Section — **UNIFORM RESIDENTIAL APPRAISAL REPORT** — File No.

COST APPROACH
ESTIMATED SITE VALUE = $
ESTIMATED REPRODUCTION COST-NEW OF IMPROVEMENTS:
Dwelling Sq. Ft. @ $ = $
Sq. Ft. @ $ = $
Garage/Carport Sq. Ft. @ $ = $
Total Estimated Cost New = $
Less Physical / Functional / External
Depreciation $ = $
Depreciated Value of Improvements = $
"As-is" Value of Site Improvements = $
INDICATED VALUE BY COST APPROACH = $

Comments on Cost Approach (such as, source of cost estimate, site value, square foot calculation and, for HUD, VA, and FmHA, the estimated remaining economic life of the property):

SALES COMPARISON ANALYSIS

ITEM	SUBJECT	COMPARABLE NO. 1	COMPARABLE NO. 2	COMPARABLE NO. 3
Address				
Proximity to Subject				
Sales Price	$	$	$	$
Price/Gross Liv. Area	$	$	$	$
Data and/or Verification Sources				

VALUE ADJUSTMENTS	DESCRIPTION	DESCRIPTION	+(−) $Adjustment	DESCRIPTION	+(−) $Adjustment	DESCRIPTION	+(−) $Adjustment
Sales or Financing Concessions							
Date of Sale/Time							
Location							
Leasehold/Fee Simple							
Site							
View							
Design and Appeal							
Quality of Construction							
Age							
Condition							
Above Grade Room Count	Total Bdrms Baths	Total Bdrms Baths		Total Bdrms Baths		Total Bdrms Baths	
Gross Living Area	Sq. Ft.	Sq. Ft.		Sq. Ft.		Sq. Ft.	
Basement & Finished Rooms Below Grade							
Functional Utility							
Heating/Cooling							
Energy Efficient Items							
Garage/Carport							
Porch, Patio, Deck, Fireplace(s), etc.							
Fence, Pool, etc.							
Net Adj. (total)		☐+ ☐− $	☐+ ☐− $		☐+ ☐− $		
Adjusted Sales Price of Comparable		$	$		$		

Comments on Sales Comparison (including the subject property's compatibility to the neighborhood, etc.):

ITEM	SUBJECT	COMPARABLE NO. 1	COMPARABLE NO. 2	COMPARABLE NO. 3
Date, Price and Data Source for prior sales within year of appraisal				

Analysis of any current agreement of sale, option, or listing of the subject property and analysis of any prior sales of subject and comparables within one year of the date of appraisal:

INDICATED VALUE BY SALES COMPARISON APPROACH $
INDICATED VALUE BY INCOME APPROACH (If Applicable) Estimated Market Rent $ /Mo. x Gross Rent Multiplier = $
This appraisal is made ☐ "as is" ☐ subject to the repairs, alterations, inspections, or conditions listed below ☐ subject to completion per plans and specifications.
Conditions of Appraisal:
Final Reconciliation:

RECONCILIATION
The purpose of this appraisal is to estimate the market value of the real property that is the subject of this report, based on the above conditions and the certification, contingent and limiting conditions, and market value definition that are stated in the attached Freddie Mac Form 439/Fannie Mae Form 1004B (Revised).
I (WE) ESTIMATE THE MARKET VALUE, AS DEFINED, OF THE REAL PROPERTY THAT IS THE SUBJECT OF THIS REPORT, AS OF
(WHICH IS THE DATE OF INSPECTION AND THE EFFECTIVE DATE OF THIS REPORT) TO BE $.

APPRAISER:	SUPERVISORY APPRAISER (ONLY IF REQUIRED):
Signature	Signature ☐ Did ☐ Did Not Inspect Property
Name	Name
Date Report Signed	Date Report Signed
State Certification # State	State Certification # State
Or State License # State	Or State License # State

Freddie Mac Form 70 6-93 — PAGE 2 OF 2 — Fannie Mae Form 1004 6-93

The Appraisal Report Form and the Valuation Process

A form appraisal report is a summary of findings. It is not the mechanism by which a value estimate is developed. Government agencies, financial institutions, insurance companies, and other organizations which process a large number of appraisals of the same type of property prefer form reports because such reports are efficient and well-suited to their needs. A form report is the most common type of report used in property appraisals for residential real estate loans.

Because of the increased use of form reports, standardized guidelines for preparing form residential appraisal reports have become essential. The Uniform Residential Appraisal Report (URAR) form, Freddie Mac 70/Fannie Mae 1004, has been revised recently to provide space for the appraiser to comply with changes in appraisal industry requirements and standards and to include additional information and analysis on the form itself that previously had to be omitted from the report or made part of the addenda material.

Guide Note 3 to the Standards of Professional Appraisal Practice of the Appraisal Institute provides guidelines for preparing residential property form appraisal reports. The guide note emphasizes that it is the appraiser's responsibility to ensure that the appropriate valuation methods and techniques have been properly employed in an appraisal reported on a form. It explains that addenda material necessary to complete the valuation process must be included. This material typically includes a value definition, the appraiser's certification, a statement of limiting conditions, maps, sketches, legal descriptions, and additional comments. A copy of Guide Note 3 is included in the appendix to this publication.

Figure 2 illustrates the complete valuation process. In a valuation for mortgage loan purposes, the subject property must be appraised in a thorough and proper manner in light of identified market conditions and in conformance with recognized ethical standards. Once this is accomplished, the findings may be communicated in several ways, one of which is through a standard appraisal report form.

The valuation process provides the guidelines and methodology needed to develop a proper value estimate. The process is accomplished by following specific steps; the number of steps required depends on the nature of the appraisal assignment and the data available to complete it. The category headings in the dark vertical bars on the left side of the form identify the various sections of the Uniform Residential Appraisal Report form; these sections reflect the steps in the valuation process, but they do not replace them. The valuation process must always be followed in defining the problem, performing market research, conducting data analysis, identifying the appraisal techniques employed, and reconciling the results into an estimate of defined value.

Figure 2. The Valuation Process

Definition of the Problem

Identification of real estate	Identification of property rights to be valued	Use of appraisal	Definition of value	Date of value estimate	Description of scope of appraisal	Other limiting conditions

Preliminary Analysis and Data Selection and Collection

General (Region, city and neighborhood)	Specific (Subject and comparables)	Competitive Supply and Demand (The subject market)
Social Economic Governmental Environmental	Site and improvements Cost and depreciation Income/expense and capitalization rate History of ownership and use of property	Inventory of competitive properties Sales and listings Vacancies and offerings Absorption rates Demand studies

Highest and Best Use Analysis

Land as though vacant
Property as improved

Specified in terms of
use, time, and market participants

Land Value Estimate

Application of the Three Approaches

Cost	Sales comparison	Income capitalization

Reconciliation of Value Indications and Final Value Estimate

Report of Defined Value

Standards of Professional Appraisal Practice Requirements

The Uniform Standards of Professional Appraisal Practice, as promulgated by The Appraisal Foundation, are recognized as the generally accepted standards of the real estate appraisal profession. Standard 1 addresses the procedures to be followed in developing a real estate appraisal and Standard 2 describes the manner in which a real estate appraisal is communicated. Selected excerpts from the printed standards document are included in the appendix. When properly developed and prepared, the revised Uniform Residential Appraisal Report form generally conforms to the requirements of Standard 2, which states in part that when reporting the results of a real estate appraisal, an appraiser must communicate each analysis, opinion, and conclusion in a manner that is not misleading.

Standards Rule 2-2 provides certain specific requirements that must be observed in the preparation of all written appraisal reports. An overview of these provisions in relation to the information required on the URAR form is provided here. Passages from the standards rule are quoted. The explanatory material that follows each passage provides specific instructions for satisfying appraisal requirements when the URAR form is used.

S.R. 2-2. *Each written real property appraisal report must:*

     a. identify and describe the real estate being appraised;

     b. identify the real property interest being appraised;

Identifying the real estate can be accomplished using a combination of a legal description, an address, a map reference, a copy of a survey or map, a property sketch, and photographs. A property sketch and photographs also provide some description of the real estate to supplement the appraiser's written comments about the physical attributes of the property. Identification of the real property rights being appraised requires a direct statement, substantiated as needed with copies of summaries of any documents setting forth encumbrances.

On the URAR form the identification of the subject property is presented in Sections A1 through A6, which call for the common address and a legal description. The real property rights being appraised are identified in Sections A14 and A15, where the appropriate box can be marked to indicate a fee simple, leasehold, PUD, or condominium interest.

     c. state the purpose of the appraisal;

     d. define the value to be estimated;

     e. set forth the effective date of the appraisal and the date of the report;

These three guidelines require clear disclosure of the "why, what, and when" surrounding the appraisal. The purpose of the appraisal generally includes both the task involved and the rationale or function of the appraisal. Defining the value to be estimated requires both an appropriately referenced definition and any comments needed to indicate to the reader how the definition is being applied. The effective date of the appraisal establishes the context for the value estimate, while the date of the report indicates whether the appraiser had a prospective, current, or retrospective view of the market conditions as of the effective date of the appraisal.

The URAR form is designed to accommodate appraisals made for real estate lending purposes. The nature, content, and use of the report provides a statement of the purpose of the appraisal. If the form is prepared for a use other than obtaining financing (such as tax assessment or litigation), the purpose should be stated in the report or an attachment.

The Statement of Limiting Conditions and Appraiser's Certification (Freddie Mac 439/Fannie Mae 1004B) identifies the value to be estimated by providing a definition of market value. If another value is to be estimated, a reference and definition must be provided in the report or an attachment.

The effective date of appraisal is set forth in Section J107 of the form. If the nature of the assignment is to provide something other than a current value estimate, then both the date for which the value estimate is effective and the date the report was prepared must be provided.

> f. describe the extent of the process of collecting, confirming, and reporting data;

When a form report is used, the significance of the appraisal problem determines in part the extent to which the process of collecting, confirming, and reporting data must be demonstrated. In most cases, the composition, intent, and contents of the form serve as the means of informing the user of the report about the extent of data collection and analysis undertaken by the appraiser.

Fannie Mae Note

The appraisal report form is designed to provide a concise format for presenting both the appraiser's description and analysis of the subject property and the valuation methodology leading to the estimate of market value. The appraiser must complete the form in a way that clearly reflects the thoroughness of his or her investigation and analysis and provides the rationale for the value estimate reached. Although the scope or extent of the valuation process is guided by Fannie Mae's appraisal report forms, the forms do not limit or control the process.

The extent of the appraiser's data collection, analysis, and reporting must be determined by the purpose and complexity of the appraisal assignment. In addition to completing the appraisal report form, the appraiser must provide any other data—either as attachments or addenda to the appraisal report form—that are necessary to support the estimate of market value. (Only appraisals that have as their purpose the estimation of market value, as defined in the Statement of Limiting Conditions and Appraiser's Certification [Form 1004B], may be used for properties that secure mortgages that will be delivered to Fannie Mae.)

> g. *set forth all assumptions and limiting conditions that affect the analyses, opinions, and conclusions;*

Assumptions and limiting conditions may be grouped together in an identified section of the report. When a residential appraisal form is used, this is accomplished by attaching the Statement of Limiting Conditions and Appraiser's Certification (Freddie Mac 439/Fannie Mae 1004B). When additional general conditions are involved, they should be identified in the report or attached with the exhibits. If the appraisal is subject to special or specific conditions that directly affect the value of the property being appraised, these conditions or assumptions must be clearly identified and referenced when the value estimate is reported.

> h. *set forth the information considered, the appraisal procedures followed, and the reasoning that supports the analyses, opinions, and conclusions;*

The appraiser must summarize the data considered and the procedures followed. Each item must be addressed in the depth and detail required by its significance to the appraisal. The appraiser must be certain that sufficient information is provided so that the client, the users of the report, and the public will be able to understand the report and will not be misled or confused.

> i. *set forth the appraiser's opinion of the highest and best use of the real estate when such an opinion is necessary and appropriate;*

A written report must contain a statement of the appraiser's opinion as to the highest and best use of the real estate being appraised, unless such an opinion is unnecessary (for example, in an appraisal for insurance purposes). If an opinion as to highest and best use is required, the reasoning behind the opinion must be included.

In relation to form reports, the key to this provision is the requirement that a properly documented analysis of highest and best use is necessary only if such an opinion is relevant to the proper valuation of the subject property. Section D49 of the URAR form addresses highest and best use by providing a choice of three responses. One box is checked when the highest and best use of the subject property is as improved as of the effective date of appraisal. If the "Present use" box is not marked, the "Other" box is appropriate and the highest and best use must be identified and explained. This can be done in the space provided in Section D53 or in a written attachment.

> j. *explain and support the exclusion of any of the usual valuation approaches;*
>
> k. *set forth any additional information that may be appropriate to show compliance with, or clearly identify and explain permitted departures from, the requirements of Standard 1;*

A written appraisal report must contain sufficient information to indicate that the appraiser has complied with the requirements of Standard 1, including the requirements governing any permitted departures from the appraisal guidelines. The amount of detail required will vary with the significance of the information to the appraisal. In the preparation of a form report, it is common practice to note in the appropriate valuation sections which approaches to value have not been included and why a specific analysis has not been developed. The need to supply additional information may require the appraiser to "think outside the form" and include as addenda all data necessary to complete the appraisal process properly and in conformance with the Uniform Standards of Professional Appraisal Practice.

l. include a signed certification in accordance with Standards Rule 2-3.

The Freddie Mac 439/Fannie Mae 1004B form includes a definition of market value, a prepared certification that generally conforms to the Uniform Standards of Professional Appraisal Practice, and a review of the general limiting conditions that apply to the value estimate. At the bottom of the certification form, space is provided for the signature and name of the appraiser(s). Space for the date of the report and state license or certification information is also included.

Conclusion

It is essential that a real estate appraiser arrive at and communicate his or her analyses and opinions in a manner that will be meaningful to the client and will not be misleading in the marketplace. When it is prepared properly and completely, the URAR form conforms to the reporting requirements of the Uniform Standards of Professional Appraisal Practice, which reflect the current standards of the appraisal industry.

Page One of the URAR Form

The first page of the Uniform Residential Appraisal Report form asks for data that describe various characteristics of the subject property and for analyses of other aspects of the property such as highest and best use. This information must be carefully recorded and closely correlated with the analysis presented in the valuation section on page two of the form. Space is provided in the upper right-hand corner of both pages to record any internal office file number or case number used by the appraiser.

| A | **Subject Identification** | In early versions of the Freddie Mac/Fannie Mae form, this section was marked "To Be Completed By Lender" and was used to provide the appraiser with the basic information needed to start the assignment. Over the years form preparation evolved and now the appraiser completes this section with data furnished by the lender or home owner. The basic information requested is not available to the appraiser unless provided by the lender or obtained by direct review of the title documents or sale contract; it is essential that the appraiser have this information at the outset of the assignment. |

A1	**Property Address**	A full and specific street address for the property to be appraised should be provided. Because this information will be used to locate the subject property, a post office box number is unacceptable. The address entered should be consistent with the address used on the sale contract and any other legal documents. The address shown in this section must appear in the same manner at the head of the Subject column in the Sales Comparison Analysis section of the form.
A2	**City**	
A3	**State**	The proper name for the city and state where the property is located must be provided. If the subject property is in a rural area, the name of the nearest city should be indicated. If abbreviations are used, they should be those that are universally recognized and accepted. Zip code maps and specific area designation numbers can be obtained from local post offices.
A4	**Zip Code**	

| A5 | **Legal Description** | A legal description is requested to help specifically identify and locate the parcel of real property being appraised. A site map is needed to determine lot size, easements, and other site data. |

Most professional appraisal firms have the resources to extract or develop a basic legal description for a property once its address has been determined. If the subject property is located in a recently completed or partially developed subdivision, however, the appraiser will need to extract the required descriptive data from current legal references, real estate tax identification numbers, and title documents.

Figure 3. Subject, Section A

Property Address **A1**			City **A2**		State **A3**	Zip Code **A4**
Legal Description **A5**					County **A6**	
Assessor's Parcel No. **A7**			Tax Year **A8**		R.E. Taxes $ **A9**	Special Assessments $ **A10**
Borrower **A11**		Current Owner **A12**			Occupant **A13** □ Owner □ Tenant □ Vacant	
Property rights appraised **A14** □ Fee Simple □ Leasehold		Project Type **A15** □ PUD □ Condominium (HUD/VA only) **A16**		HOA$ /Mo.		
Neighborhood or Project Name **A17**					Map Reference **A18**	Census Tract **A19**
Sales Price $ **A20**	Date of Sale **A21**			Description and $ amount of loan charges/concessions to be paid by seller **A22**		
Lender/Client **A23**		Address **A24**				
Appraiser **A25**		Address **A26**				

SUBJECT

| **A6** | **County** | Identification of the county in which the subject property is located is important because it further identifies the property and suggests geographical and jurisdictional parameters for conducting research and analysis. The appraiser records the full name of the county in the space provided. |

| **A7** | **Assessor's Parcel No.** | The assessor's parcel number is used by the local assessor to identify the property for the tax rolls; it can also be used to obtain tax and other financial information concerning the property. The assessor's parcel number is not a legal description and may not be substituted for a legal description. It is, however, often used in the real estate industry for quick identification of a property when a legal description is not required. The appraiser records the number to verify that the tax information provided corresponds with the assessor's identification of the subject property. |

| **A8** | **Tax Year** | The effective tax year or years covered by the property taxes indicated on the form should be entered in this space. |

| **A9** | **Real Estate Taxes** | The dollar amount of annual property taxes currently levied against the subject property should be entered here. The actual amount paid may by obtained from public records at the tax assessor's office, the owner's tax bill, or title documents. |

The appraiser studies this information for a variety of reasons. Taxation is often a significant variable when comparing one neighborhood with another. Property tax considerations may differentiate otherwise similar neighborhoods and are therefore a factor in setting boundaries in the collection of sales data.

| **A10** | **Special Assessments** | Special assessments are special levies imposed by a government taxing agency for a specific purpose for a limited period of time. Normally such assessments are made for public improvements such as the installation of utilities or roads. The amount of an assessment is based on the perceived benefits to the property, not the cost of providing the benefit to the property. Special assessments are listed separately on tax bills and should be studied for their impact on the value and marketability of the affected properties during the period they are levied and immediately afterwards. |

If a special assessment is in force as of the effective date of appraisal, the total amount is entered on the form. Additional information on the assessment and its impact on the subject should be provided in the appropriate description and analysis sections of the report. Special assessments that relate to home owners' fees are not entered here, but in Section A16.

A11	**Borrower**
A12	**Current Owner**
A13	**Current Occupant**

First the appraiser enters the name of the individual or entity applying for a loan on the subject property—i.e., the borrower. This may or may not be the current owner or occupant. The borrower may be the purchaser or the current owner seeking to refinance the property. The name of the current owner is entered next. The appraiser needs this information to research public and legal documents. The name and telephone number of the occupant should be recorded in Section A12 and the appropriate box "Owner," "Tenant," or "Vacant" should be checked in Section A13. These entries supply the information necessary to gain access to the subject property for purposes of inspection.

In the event of a sale, the appraiser should determine if the current occupant is a tenant, the seller, or another participant in the subject transaction. Tenant occupancy may be an important value consideration. The appraiser should quantify its effect with regard to neighborhood use trends and property condition and consider it again in the valuation section if the income approach is applied.

A14   **Property Rights Appraised**

The appraiser must determine or be made aware of the property rights to be appraised. In most instances, a fee simple ownership is being valued and the "Fee Simple" box should be checked. If another type of interest is being appraised, an attachment explaining and describing the exact form of ownership or interest should be included with the form report. The appraiser must distinguish between fee simple and leasehold interests.

Fee simple interest is the transferable right of property ownership most often appraised for mortgage lending purposes. In a fee simple estate, the property owner enjoys the right to utilize, encumber, and dispose of the property freely and at will, subject only to basic ownership restrictions. Because it is the most common form of real estate ownership and will most often be specified as the property right to be appraised, it requires no additional explanation within the body of the form report.

Leasehold interest is the right to use and occupy real property by virtue of a lease agreement. A tenant enjoys these rights for a stipulated time period, subject to payment of rent and other conditions. Leasehold property rights are rarely appraised for residential mortgage loan purposes. The valuation of a leasehold may require complex analysis, so the appraiser should be prepared to develop a thorough, clear, and detailed narrative description of all terms and conditions and provide it as an attachment to the report.

The "Leasehold" box should be checked if the house being appraised is on leased land. Although this is an uncommon situation, there are parts of the country where ownership of a single-family residence is not held in fee simple. In these cases, the owner of the building is required to pay "ground rent" and the property may revert to the landowner at the end of the lease term. Such a situation may have a negative impact on property value. The terms of the ground lease should be identified and the effect of the lease should be analyzed in a narrative attached to the appraisal form.

Project Type— PUD—Condominium

If the property being appraised is situated within a planned unit development (PUD) or condominium project, the appraiser should check the appropriate box.

A PUD may be defined as a zoning alternative rather than a type of residence. A planned unit development permits more flexibility in land use than is possible where zoning laws provide for lot-by-lot utilization. In a PUD, housing units can be built on lots smaller than those usually required for residential construction. In exchange for the right to build at higher densities, the developer sets aside some land to be used by the community or the home owners' association. In PUD projects streets, landscaping, and public facilities can be designed to create a total living environment. Residences may be in the form of single-family homes, townhouses, multifamily buildings, or a combination of these styles.

Fannie Mae and Freddie Mac will accept appraisals of detached condominium units reported on the URAR form provided that 1) the project does not contain any common area improvements other than greenbelts, private streets, and parking areas; and 2) the appraiser includes an adequate description of the project and details concerning the home owners' association fees and project maintenance. The Department of Housing and Urban Development (HUD) and the Department of Veterans Affairs (VA) accept all types of individual condominium unit appraisals reported on the URAR.

A condominium is defined as a form of ownership created by special real estate laws which permit estates to individual dwelling units to be established within a larger property entity. A condominium unit is a separate ownership and title is held by an individual owner. The owner possesses the three-dimensional space within the outer walls, roof or ceiling, and floors of the dwelling unit and, along with other unit owners, has an individual interest in common areas including the land and public portions of the building or buildings such as the foundation, the outer walls, and all parking and recreational facilities.

As in a PUD project, a home owners' association is created to control the use and maintenance of the common areas and the condominium project is governed by a board of directors elected by the individual owners.

HOA$/Mo.

This section is completed if the property being appraised qualifies as a condominium or PUD and the owner is subject to home owners' dues for the use of common areas and amenities. The monthly dollar amount assessed to the individual unit is entered here. The appraiser must determine whether the home owners' association fees are reasonable in comparison to the fees paid by owners of units in other projects of similar quality and design. The monthly common area charges are compared to the charges allocated to similar units in competing projects.

Home owners' associations may also, from time to time, impose special assessments on unit owners for repairs or improvements not covered in the monthly dues. In this case, the appraiser reports the amount of the special assessment and comments on its effect on the subject's value and marketability. The theory of substitution suggests that a prospective buyer will not pay the same price for a unit with high monthly fees that offers the same amenities as units with lower fees.

Appraisal Note

Sometimes a developer retains ownership of the project's recreational facilities and leases them on a long-term basis to the home owners' association, which imposes a prorated charge on unit owners. Under the recreational lease, the charge to each individual unit owner is usually small, but the annual return to the developer can be substantial. Each owner pays a fixed monthly charge and many leases provide for annual increases tied to a cost-of-living index. This practice has been abused, however, and attempts are being made to restrict the use of recreational leases. The FHA will not finance a residential project that is subject to a recreational lease. For appraisal purposes, therefore, properties with and without recreational leases cannot be directly compared.

A17

Neighborhood or Project Name

Sometimes a neighborhood or a portion of a neighborhood is identified by a name denoting its original development (e.g., St. James Estates), a geographical feature (e.g., Atlas Peak), or some other distinctive attribute. Most PUD and condominium projects have names. If the subject property is situated in a neighborhood or area with a commonly known title or project name, it should be identified here. Such information can help the appraiser begin to establish criteria for the neighborhood description. The named neighborhood or project may or may not have the same boundaries as those indicated in the neighborhood description (Section B), but it should fall within the boundaries of the neighborhood as described in Section B37. Many residential neighborhoods are not associated with a specific name. In such instances the appraiser may enter "N/A" (not applicable).

A18

Map Reference

The map reference provided should relate to the system most commonly used by the appraisal and lending communities within the local market area. For example, reference may be made to maps used by local tax assessors and government census maps. The appraiser must include the source of the map and its identification number.

A19

Census Tract

The appraiser must record the appropriate designation number for any subject property located within a formally assigned census tract. If the property is not located in a designated census tract, the notation "N/A" should be entered in the space to show that a census tract number is not applicable.

| A20 | Sales Price | In the case of a property transfer, the total acquisition price should be specified. Many sales contracts include addenda to the original purchase terms. The sales price reported here should reflect the terms of the last or most recent addendum to the sales contract. The sales price shown here must correspond exactly with the amount recorded in the Subject column of the Sales Comparison Analysis section (H74) on the second page of the report form. (See the discussion of Section A22 for information on the treatment of sales concessions and other factors that may influence the purchase price.)

The appraiser must provide an entry on this line. If the appraisal is requested for a transaction other than a purchase, "N/A," "Refinance," or "None" may be recorded.

In the appraisal of one- to four-family residential properties, all prior sales of the subject property occurring within one year of the effective date of valuation must be identified and considered. |
|---|---|---|

A21	Date of Sale	If a property transfer has occurred, the exact date of sale shown in the purchase contract should be provided. The date of purchase may also be extracted from the property transfer deed or the mortgage loan documents. When confirmed, the date of sale and source of verification should be specified, e.g., "July 14, 1993 - Sales Contract" or "August 10, 1992 - Escrow Closed." If there was no sale, an entry of "N/A" (not applicable) should be recorded.

| A22 | Description of $ amount of loan charges/concessions to be paid by seller | The appraiser must be aware of all loan fees or points, settlement charges, discounts to the sale price, interest rate buydowns, condominium or PUD fees, and other charges to be paid by the seller as a requirement of the contract or terms of sale. The dollar amount and type of charge should be indicated on the form in the space provided. Additional details or explanations may be included in an attachment to the report.

Sales concessions usually consist of considerations in the contract that may have an effect on the valuation of the subject property. The appraiser should be informed of each component of personal property that is included in the sales contract. Information concerning the amount, interest rate, and term of any junior liens should be provided. Any credit of cash or labor granted by the buyer or seller that may have affected the sale price should be specified. A "deferred delivery" arrangement between the buyer and seller will tend to affect the agreed-upon acquisition price.

Fannie Mae reporting guidelines require that the lender provide the appraiser with all financing data and sales concessions that have been granted by anyone associated with the transaction. Information that must be disclosed includes items such as:
- Settlement charges
- Loan fees or charges
- Discounts to the sale price
- Interest rate buydowns or other below-market rate financing |
|---|---|---|

- Refunds or credits
- Absorption of monthly payments
- Assignment of rent payments
- Non-realty items that were included in the transaction

Fannie Mae Note

To ensure that the impact of sales and financing concessions is properly acknowledged, not only is the appraiser required to make appropriate adjustments in analyzing the property's value, but the lender is also responsible for adjusting the sale price to take any "excess" contributions into consideration. For underwriting purposes, the lender must make a negative adjustment to the property's sale price to reflect the amount of any contributions that exceed the maximum allowed. Then the loan-to-value ratio is calculated using the reduced sale price or the appraised value, whichever is less.

Standards Note

Guide Note 2 to the Standards of Professional Appraisal Practice of the Appraisal Institute addresses cash equivalency in accordance with Standards Rule 1-2(b). Unacceptable practices are stated as follows:

1. *Failure to accurately report the specific terms of any existing or proposed financing of the subject property, when such financing has an impact on the appraisal problem. (See S.R. 1-2(b)).*
2. *Failure to estimate and report the effect of favorable or unfavorable financing terms on value. (See S.R. 1-2(b)).*
3. *Failure to analyze and make appropriate adjustments to a comparable sale that included favorable or unfavorable financing terms as of the date of sale, when comparing the sale to the property being appraised. (See S.R. 1-2(b)).*
4. *Failure to state that financing data on a comparable sale is not available despite diligent investigation, and that reliance on the particular sale is thus limited. (See S.R. 1-4(b) (iii)).*

| A23 | **Lender/Client** | The full name and street or mailing address of the lender or client should be entered. In most instances, or unless otherwise specified, the lender is the appraiser's client. |
| A24 | **Address** | |

| A25 | **Appraiser** | The full name and street or mailing address of the appraiser who has performed the appraisal and signed the report should be recorded. |
| A26 | **Address** | |

B | **Neighborhood Description**

Neighborhood analysis allows the appraiser to judge a property relative to its surroundings. Identification of the neighborhood also helps to limit the scope of the search for data and allows the appraiser to determine the usefulness of comparable sales data. The sale prices of comparable properties located in the same neighborhood as the subject property usually require little or no adjustment for location.

Neighborhood analysis also helps the appraiser assess the overall stability of a residential area. It provides a basis for determining the position of properties in a neighborhood's overall life cycle and may indicate future land uses and value trends for neighborhood properties.

In identifying and discussing neighborhood conditions, the appraiser should remain objective and impartially describe all special amenities or detrimental conditions. Any changes or observed trends that may influence the value of the properties within the neighborhood must be explained. The appraiser should also comment on any inherent market resistance arising from the known presence of an environmental hazard or other negative factors.

B27 | **Location**

The neighborhood description is critical in establishing the applicability of the sales selected as comparables and judging whether or not the subject property is typical for the neighborhood. *Urban* generally identifies a mature neighborhood with a concentration of population; an urban neighborhood is typically found within city limits or commonly identified with a city. *Suburban* refers to a neighborhood of complementary properties with a less concentrated population than is typically found in an urban neighborhood. *Rural* areas are generally those exhibiting relatively slow growth with development of less than 25%. Properties located in rural neighborhoods are eligible for Fannie Mae loans only when the primary dwelling (including garage) represents 70% or more of the total appraised value.

Traditionally, rural properties such as farms and ranches are more land-intensive than other residential properties. In addition, the adequacy of features such as utilities and road access can vary widely. If the "Rural" box is checked, the appraiser should indicate in the neighborhood comments the property's suitability for a regular residential loan.

An appropriate description of the subject property's environment reflects the appraiser's judgment and may determine the suitability of the properties chosen as comparables in the Sales Comparison Analysis section of the form. For example, if the "Rural" box is checked, it might be appropriate to use comparable sales of houses located a greater distance away from the subject than if the "Suburban" category were chosen. If the "Urban" box is checked, the appraiser will be expected to describe and compare specific locational factors such as local traffic concentration and proximity to schools and shopping.

Figure 4. Neighborhood, Section B

NEIGHBORHOOD

								Present land use % **B35**	Land use change **B36**
Location	**B27**	☐ Urban	☐ Suburban	☐ Rural	**Predominant occupancy** **B33**	**Single family housing** **B34**		One family ☐	Not likely ☐
Built up	**B28**	☐ Over 75%	☐ 25-75%	☐ Under 25%	☐ Owner	PRICE $(000) AGE (yrs)		2-4 family ☐	In process ☐
Growth rate	**B29**	☐ Rapid	☐ Stable	☐ Slow	☐ Tenant	Low		Multi-family ☐	Likely ☐
Property values	**B30**	☐ Increasing	☐ Stable	☐ Declining	☐ Vacant (0-5%)	High		Commercial ☐	To:
Demand/supply	**B31**	☐ Shortage	☐ In balance	☐ Over supply	☐ Vacant (over 5%)	Predominant		( )	
Marketing time	**B32**	☐ Under 3 mos.	☐ 3-6 mos.	☐ Over 6 mos.					

Note: Race and the racial composition of the neighborhood are not appraisal factors.

Neighborhood boundaries and characteristics: **B37** _____

Factors that affect the marketability of the properties in the neighborhood (proximity to employment and amenities, employment stability, appeal to market, etc.): **B38**

_____

_____

_____

Market conditions in the subject neighborhood (including support for the above conclusions related to the trend of property values, demand/supply, and marketing time...such as data on competitive properties for sale in the neighborhood, description of the prevalence of sales and financing concessions, etc.): **B39**

_____

_____

_____

| B28 | Built up | This section is concerned with the percentage of improved area of all building types within the subject neighborhood or other identified environment. The percentage of area not built up is the portion that is vacant at the time of the appraisal but is available for use and potential development. As indicated in the discussion of location (B27), there may be an obvious relationship between the percentage of improvement and the property's location within an urban, suburban, or rural district.

The appraiser should comment if the subject is located in an apparently underdeveloped area and explain any inconsistency between the extent of development and the neighborhood character indicated in Section B27. |

| B29 | Growth rate | To complete this entry, the appraiser needs to make a judgment concerning the growth of residential development in the subject neighborhood in relation to normal market factors. If a slow growth rate is indicated, an explanation concerning any potential adverse effect on the marketability of the property being appraised should be provided in Section B38. |

| B30 | Property values | Here the appraiser records an opinion regarding current trends in market prices. If a declining value pattern is identified, the appraiser should provide supporting market evidence and explain any anticipated or resultant effect on the value of the subject property.

From an underwriting standpoint, property values ideally should be stable or increasing. If they are declining, the appraiser should comment on the reasons for the decline and the probability of this trend continuing. Properties in such areas must be viewed with great care. Because the reasons for a decline in values and the probability of its continuance are key considerations in developing a proper value estimate, the appraiser should be ready to show the logic behind any estimate of declining value. |

| B31 | Demand/supply | Demand and supply observations should be limited to an analysis of residential properties located within the subject neighborhood. A check in the "In balance" box indicates an average marketing period for the typical home in the immediate neighborhood. If "Shortage" is checked, demand currently exceeds supply and an identifiable increase or appreciation in value can be anticipated. If "Oversupply" is marked, the appraiser should provide market evidence to explain the impact of the oversupply on the value of the subject property. |

B32	**Marketing time**	In this section the appraiser estimates the potential marketing time of a typical residential property in the subject neighborhood. There is a strong interrelationship among growth rate, property values, supply and demand conditions, and marketing time. For example, stabilized to increasing property values may be the result of a temporary decrease in supply, which leads to a relatively short marketing period. The appraiser's observations of market influences must be carefully correlated and reported. Any inconsistencies among inter-related conditions should be fully addressed in the report.

B33	**Predominant occupancy**	The appraiser must identify the predominant type of occupancy and estimate the percentage of vacancy. This refers to the occupancy of residential properties only. For example, if the neighborhood consists of two-family properties, 90% of which are owner-occupied, the "Owner" box should be checked. If there is a relatively small prepon-derance of owners over tenants, say 60% owners versus 40% tenants, this fact should be reported separately in the market conditions comments section (B39) because the long-term desirability of the neighborhood as a single-family residential environment could be adversely affected.

B34	**Single-family housing—Price and Age**	In completing this section the appraiser need not consider isolated extremes within the individual price or age ranges. The predominant value recorded should reflect the appraiser's best determination of the mode, i.e., the most frequently occurring residential sale price within the subject market area. If the subject's sale price or indicated value is at the extreme upper end or outside the ranges established, the appraiser is expected to comment on the divergence and offer an opinion as to the anticipated effect on the property's marketability and overall appeal.

Similar consideration should be given to the age range for proper-ties in the neighborhood. It is important that the age of the subject property fall within the general age range of properties in the neighbor-hood. Neighborhoods are usually developed over a relatively short span of time, so most dwelling units will fall within similar age brackets.

B35	**Present land use %**	In this section the appraiser estimates the percentage of each property type in the neighborhood. Typically, dwellings maintain their value best when situated in neighborhoods of other residential properties. If commercial uses or other land uses that could harm residential values are identified, their proximity and influence on the subject property should be explained. If land is used for a purpose other than the four types of uses specified on the form, the appraiser should indicate the property type and percentage of use and address the effect of the use under "factors that affect marketability" in Section B38.

If the neighborhood contains a measurable amount of vacant land available for development, the appraiser should record the percentage of vacant land. The total of all land uses must equal 100%.

B36	**Land use change**	Here the appraiser judges the likelihood of a change in significant land use or uses within the subject neighborhood. If a change is "likely" or "in process," the new or eventual land use should be recorded in the space provided. A change in land use could have a detrimental impact on residential values. This possibility should be fully explained in relation to the subject property's potential marketability and overall buyer appeal; the appraiser's comments are usually prepared as an addendum to the report.

B37	**Neighborhood boundaries and characteristics**	The neighborhood comprises the area of complementary properties nearest to the subject property. Its boundaries are determined by measuring factors that prospective buyers consider when purchasing properties.

In defining neighborhood boundaries, the appraiser may analyze changes in topographical features such as hills or bodies of water or consider changes in land use identified by zoning, tax rates, and other government regulations. Neighborhood boundaries may reflect changes in the predominant age, quality, style, price, and occupancy of residential dwellings or be based on proximity to external influences that have either a negative or positive impact on the residential area.

In this section the appraiser identifies the physical boundaries of the subject neighborhood. In urban and suburban areas, it is common to use street names, points of interest, and natural barriers to describe neighborhood boundaries. For example, the description of an urban neighborhood might read, "The generally accepted neighborhood boundaries are Hawkins Street on the north, St. John Seminary on the west, March Road on the south, and Interstate 220 on the east." In rural settings the identification of neighborhood boundaries may depend more on natural and jurisdictional barriers—e.g., "for the purposes of this appraisal assignment, the neighborhood includes the area south of the Gila Mountain Range, east of the San Carlos Indian Reservation, north of U.S. 70, and west of Bonita Creek." In any case the neighborhood boundaries reported in this section should be easy for the reader to find on the location map attached to the report.

To complete this section properly, the appraiser is also expected to identify the common characteristics of the neighborhood that can influence properties within its boundaries favorably and unfavorably.

B38	**Factors that affect the marketability of the properties in the neighborhood (proximity to employment and amenities, employment stability, appeal to market, etc.)**	Here the appraiser describes the social, economic, governmental, and environmental forces that impact the subject neighborhood. The stability of the local economy; the adequacy, quality, and proximity of public services and recreational facilities; and the overall attractiveness and condition of the individual properties in the neighborhood have a direct bearing on a neighborhood's competitive appeal. In this space the appraiser can provide a further explanation of previously described characteristics and address other factors that may have a favorable or unfavorable impact on property values presently or in the future. Negative neighborhood factors that create external obsolescence are considered here and in Section F69, in the depreciation section of the Cost Approach, Section G70, and on the Location line, Section H79, of the Sales Comparison Analysis on page two of the form.

Market conditions in the subject neighborhood...

The appraiser should use this space to discuss market conditions and trends which reflect the positive and negative factors that influence residential property values in the subject neighborhood. Marketing time and the supply of and demand for housing have a direct impact on property values and the methods of financing available. The appraiser must identify the financing practices prevalent in the area as well as the specific financing terms of the subject (if applicable) to identify the differences between the two.

The comments presented here should be consistent with the information given in previous sections of the form report. Details concerning loan charges and concessions are reported in Section A22; the proper adjustment amounts for these factors can be entered in Section H77 and further discussed in Section H98.

The appraiser should also use this space to summarize the neighborhood analysis, emphasizing the specific features that have the greatest influence on property values in the subject neighborhood.

Appraisal Note

As a review, the factors that tend to increase value in a residential neighborhood are:

- Convenient access to educational, religious, health, and recreational facilities
- The presence of neighborhood organizations such as home owners' associations and civic groups
- Visual appeal
- Adequate transportation facilities and good access to major roads and freeway systems
- Advantageous topographical and geographical features
- Good neighborhood planning and adequate utilities
- Compatible land uses and protective zoning

After assessing the neighborhood's advantages, the appraiser should consider factors that tend to affect value adversely. Negative factors include:

- Declining sale prices of surrounding properties
- High vacancy and turnover rate
- Vandalism or litter
- The emergence of nonconforming uses in the area
- Pollution from smoke, noise, and heavy traffic
- The proximity of hazardous waste materials
- Factors such as a lack of zoning protection, increasing taxes, poor planning, congestion, an incompatible mix of architectural styles, a lack of trees or landscaping, insufficient street parking, and poor maintenance

The purpose of neighborhood analysis is to identify the area, based on common characteristics or trends, that is subject to the same influences as the subject property. In neighborhood analysis the appraiser considers the influence of social, economic, governmental, and environmental forces on property values in the subject neighborhood.

To perform a neighborhood analysis, the appraiser should collect pertinent data, make a visual inspection of the neighborhood to observe its physical characteristics and boundaries, identify land uses and note any signs that they are changing, and rate the relative quality of the neighborhood. The results of the analysis will help the appraiser to understand market preferences and price patterns; reach conclusions about the highest and best use of the subject site; define the area from which to select comparables; examine the effect of different locations within the neighborhood; determine the influence of nearby land uses; and identify any other value influences affecting the neighborhood. The appraiser should extend his or her search of the subject market area as far as necessary to ensure that all significant influences affecting the value of the property are reflected in the appraisal report.

In summary, the URAR form requires the appraiser to describe the neighborhood boundaries and to provide a narrative description of the favorable and unfavorable factors that affect marketability and market conditions. Appraisers should use their best judgment in establishing and describing neighborhood boundaries. The limits of a neighborhood can be identified by various physical, jurisdictional, economic, or other characteristics.

Figure 5. PUD, Section C

PUD

Project information for PUDs (If applicable) — Is the developer/builder in control of the Home Owners' Association (HOA)? C40 ☐ Yes ☐ No C42

Approximate total number of units in the subject project C41 _____. Approximate total number of units for sale in the subject project _____.

Describe common elements and recreational facilities: C43

24

C	**PUD Project Information**

As previously discussed, a planned unit development is composed of individually owned properties (lots) with certain common areas that are shared by all property owners within the development. To estimate the value of an individual PUD unit, the appraiser must analyze documents pertaining to the ownership and use of the property and the financial health of the project. These documents may include information on CC&Rs (conditions, covenants, and restrictions) and the formula for determining the ownership percentages of common areas, operating and reserve budgets, monthly home owners' association fees, and any special assessments.

PUD developments vary greatly in size, in types of improvements, and in the types and number of amenities. Some PUD projects have minimal monthly fees or no fees at all; they exist simply to control certain physical or use features of the individual properties. Other PUDs have many commonly owned amenities managed by a home owners' association and charge substantial monthly dues.

The appraiser must determine whether the subject's CC&Rs and fees are reasonable in comparison to the fees charged for units in other projects of similar quality and design. Special assessments also may have an impact on the marketability of a PUD property. As mentioned previously, the theory of substitution suggests that a prospective purchaser will not pay the same price for a unit with high charges that offers the same amenities as units with lower charges.

Appraisal Note

Fannie Mae describes a planned unit development (PUD) as a project that consists of common property and improvements that are owned and maintained by an owners' association for the benefit and use of owners of the individual units within the project. For a project to qualify as a PUD, the home owners' association must require automatic, nonseverable membership for each individual unit owner and provide for mandatory assessments. Zoning is not the basis for classifying a project as a PUD.

C40 Is the developer/ builder in control of the Home Owners' Association (HOA)?

Occasionally a project developer/builder may retain interest in the common area improvements after construction is completed. This arrangement can create complications and may lead to certain underwriting problems. If such an arrangement exists, the "yes" box must be checked and an addendum describing the terms and other details of the arrangement should be attached to the appraisal report.

C41 Approximate total number of units in the subject project

The appraiser records the total number of living units in the project. For a fully constructed project, this includes all existing dwellings. In a partially completed project, this number reflects all existing dwellings plus all planned units. If the project is incomplete, the appraiser should provide further information on the status of the construction, an estimated completion schedule, and any other pertinent details on the project in Section B39 of the neighborhood analysis.

| C42 | **Approximate total number of units for sale in the subject project** | The total number of units available for purchase in the subject project as of the effective date of appraisal is identified and reported. The appraiser should determine whether the number of units available is typical, higher than typical, or lower than typical as compared to competing projects. A further explanation is needed in Section B38 or B39 if the number of units is either higher or lower than typical. |

| C43 | **Describe common elements and recreational facilities** | On this line the appraiser describes the general common area and recreational facilities provided in the project. The general common area is the property owned jointly by all unit owners. It ordinarily includes land and structures that are not part of the individual unit properties. The size and number of improvements such as greenbelts, community buildings, swimming pools, saunas, and tennis courts must be in proportion to the overall size and character of the project and comparable to those provided at competing developments.

One common defect that can cause incurable obsolescence to residential properties within a PUD is excessive development of amenities. The cost of using and maintaining elaborate, oversized improvements must be passed on to the individual owners in the form of high home owners' association dues. |

D	**Site Description**	A site analysis is a careful study of data on the subject property in relation to neighborhood characteristics that create, enhance, or detract from the utility or marketability of the site as compared with competing land parcels. To maintain maximum value, the site should be of a size, shape, and topography that is generally acceptable in the market area. It should also have utilities, street improvements, and other amenities that are competitive with those of other properties. Because easements and encroachments may either detract from or enhance a site's marketability, the appraiser should comment on the effect of their presence or absence.
D44	**Dimensions**	The dimensions of the subject site are to be listed (width x length x width x length). Most lenders require that a site map be attached and referenced.
D45	**Site area**	The total land area must be recorded, expressed in square feet or acres. The measure used should be consistent with that used in the left-hand portion of the Site and View sections (H81 and H82) of the Sales Comparison Analysis. If only part of the site can be designated "usable area," the area of this portion should be calculated and the site conditions should be explained.
D46	**Corner Lot**	The appraiser checks the appropriate box to indicate whether or not the subject site is situated on a corner. Any additional comments should be made in Section D53.
D47	**Specific zoning classification and description**	The specific zoning category and major permitted uses should be indicated. The designation assigned by local zoning code should be written in full—e.g., "R-1 Residential - Single Family." A major function of the zoning classification is to identify the residential density allowed.
D48	**Zoning compliance**	If the present improvements conform to zoning regulations, the appraiser should check the "Legal" box. An entry of "Legal nonconforming (Grandfathered use)" generally suggests that the existing structure has been allowed to stand, but if it is demolished or substantially damaged by fire or another catastrophe, the property may only be redeveloped for a use permitted under the present zoning.

"Illegal" use describes an existing structure that does not conform to current local zoning regulations and is not designated as legal nonconforming. "No zoning" refers to improved properties located where no zoning requirements are in force.

If the improvements do not represent a legal, conforming use under the current zoning regulations, the appraiser must address this fact and discuss how it affects the marketability and value of the subject property in the space provided for site comments, Section D53. |

Figure 6. Site, Section D

SITE		
Dimensions D44		Topography D52
Site area D45		Size
Specific zoning classification and description D47		Shape
Zoning compliance D48 ☐ Legal ☐ Legal nonconforming (Grandfathered use) ☐ Illegal ☐ No zoning		Drainage
Highest & best use as improved: D49 ☐ Present use ☐ Other use (explain)		View

Utilities D50	Public	Other	Off-site improvements D51	Type	Public	Private	Landscaping
Electricity	☐		Street		☐	☐	Driveway Surface
Gas	☐		Curb/gutter		☐	☐	Apparent easements
Water	☐		Sidewalk		☐	☐	FEMA Special Flood Hazard Area ☐ Yes ☐ No
Sanitary sewer	☐		Street lights		☐	☐	FEMA Zone _____ Map Date
Storm sewer	☐		Alley		☐	☐	FEMA Map No.

D46 Corner Lot ☐ Yes ☐ No

Comments (apparent adverse easements, encroachments, special assessments, slide areas, illegal or nonconforming zoning use, etc.): D53

| **D49** | **Highest and best use as improved** | The entry most often checked here is "Present use." If "Other use" is marked, the appraiser must document and explain the reasoning supporting an alternative use. |

The entry most often checked here is "Present use." If "Other use" is marked, the appraiser must document and explain the reasoning supporting an alternative use.

Guide Note 3 to the Standards of Professional Appraisal Practice of the Appraisal Institute explains that in determining a site's highest and best use, the appraiser tests each potential use to determine if it is physically possible, legally permissible, and financially feasible. The tests are generally applied in this order, and any use that fails to meet one of the tests is eliminated from further consideration. Of the uses that remain, the one that is the most profitable is selected as the highest and best use of the site as though vacant.

Fannie Mae guidelines stipulate that, if the analysis of comparable sales demonstrates that the improvements are reasonably typical and compatible with market demand for the neighborhood and the present improvements contribute value to the subject property so that its value is greater than the estimated vacant site value, the appraiser should consider the existing use as reasonable and report it as the highest and best use. If, on the other hand, the current improvements clearly do not represent the highest and best use of the site, the appraiser must indicate this fact in the appraisal report.

The appraiser's highest and best use analysis of the subject property should consider the property as it is improved. This analysis recognizes the fact that the existing improvements should continue in use until it is financially feasible to renovate or demolish them.

D50   Utilities

Under this heading the appraiser identifies five types of public or alternative (other) utility services. If "other" utilities are indicated, a statement must be included explaining their acceptability within the market area, their legality, and their effect on the value of the subject property.

For a residence to maintain maximum value, its utilities must meet community standards. If public sewer or water facilities are not available, then community or private well and septic facilities must be available for use by the subject property.

D51   Off-site Improvements

The appraiser should provide a brief description for each of the five categories of off-site improvements and indicate if their maintenance is public or private. Under "Type" the appraiser identifies the specific surface material or construction component—e.g., asphalt street, concrete sidewalk.

A property maintains its maximum value when it is accessed by a publicly maintained, all-weather street. If the dwelling is on a street that is community-owned or privately owned, information concerning maintenance must be provided in the comments section (D53) or in an addendum.

Fannie Mae guidelines stipulate that the property improvements should front on a publicly dedicated and maintained street that meets community standards and is generally accepted by area residents.

If the property fronts on a community-owned or privately owned and maintained street, there should be an adequate, legally enforceable agreement for maintenance of the street. A street that does not meet city, county, or state standards frequently requires extensive maintenance, and property values may decline if it is not regularly maintained. If a property fronts on a street that is not typical of those found in the community, the appraiser must comment on how this fact affects the marketability and value of the property being appraised.

Physical Characteristics

In this section the appraiser describes briefly the key features of the subject site as compared with other sites in the neighborhood. Most of these features may be evaluated by visual inspection.

Topography. The contour and surface features of the land should be described with terms such as "level," "gentle unslope," or "steep downslope."

Size. The lot size is described in comparison to other sites in the neighborhood. The terms "typical" and "average" are appropriate for lots that fall within the normal size range. If the site is described as "larger than typical" or "smaller than average," additional comments concerning the potential effect of this feature on the value of the site may be required.

Shape. Shape refers to the lot's general configuration, such as "rectangular," "triangular," "flag," or "irregular." The shape of a lot affects its value differently in different neighborhoods. In some areas irregularity of shape may decrease value; in other areas there appears to be little difference between the value of regularly and irregularly shaped sites as long as the lot is suitable for residential development. If the irregular shape of a parcel results in increased construction costs, however, land value will probably be decreased. The description entered here should correspond to the general shape of the site as it is depicted on the site map attachment.

Drainage. Drainage systems vary in type and complexity, depending on site contours and the position of the improvements. All are designed to carry moisture away from the structure's foundation and to prevent soil erosion. Drainage is described as "adequate" or "inadequate" based on the appraiser's visual inspection of the site. If drainage is described as "inadequate," a detailed explanation of the problem and its location on the site must be presented in the comments section (D53) or in an addendum.

Information relative to flood conditions, that is, the property's likelihood of flood exposure, is to be provided under "FEMA Special Flood Hazard Area" at the bottom of Section D52.

Appraisal Note

The topography, shape, size, and drainage of the site are equally important. Steep slopes that cause erosion make landscaping difficult to maintain; impaired access to the property itself or to a garage are generally seen as unfavorable conditions. Drainage pipes must be directed away from the improvements to prevent water from collecting in or around buildings. The need for sidewalks, curbs and gutters, streetlights, and alleys depends on local custom; if they are typical in the community, they should be present on the subject site. The appraiser must comment on any adverse conditions and address their effect on the marketability and value of the property being appraised.

View. The appraiser describes the predominant view from the property, such as "street," "neighborhood," "central city," or "ocean." The appraiser should determine if the view is "superior," "typical," or "inferior" to the neighborhood average and note whether the view is a value consideration in the analysis of the site.

Landscaping. The site's landscaping is described in comparison with competing residential sites in the subject's market area. "Typical" or "average" can be used to describe the neighborhood norm; an entry of "superior" or "inferior" indicates that the landscaping is above or below the standard for competing properties in the neighborhood.

Driveway Surface. The appraiser should note the type of surface material used such as "concrete," "macadam," "gravel," or "dirt." The driveway's adequacy for auto ingress and egress to the parking area should also be noted. If there is no driveway, the appropriate entry is "none." In this case the appraiser should note whether the lack of a driveway adversely affects the value or marketability of the property.

Apparent easements. The type of easement or easements applicable to the site such as "drainage," "power," or "property access" should be recorded. Because some easements may not be visible, the appraiser should review the title documents to identify any recorded easements in effect as of the date of the appraisal. Such information may also be obtained from property owners or sales agents. When easements are known but cannot be observed by visual inspection, the appraiser should note the source of the information obtained.

Typically, easements on residential sites are designated for utilities, telephone and television cable, drainage, and similar services. Normally these easements are situated in such a way that site use is minimally affected. In most cases they have little or no effect on the value or marketability of the site. Nevertheless, the appraiser must analyze and address any adverse effects that apparent or known easements may have on the subject property.

FEMA Special Flood Hazard Area, FEMA Zone/Map Date, FEMA Map No. The Federal Emergency Management Agency (FEMA) documents and publishes lists of districts identified as special flood hazard areas. To determine whether the subject lies within an identified flood hazard zone, the appraiser must refer to a flood hazard boundary map, a flood insurance rate map, or information provided by a local agency that identifies special hazard areas. If part or all of the structure is situated in a flood hazard area, "Yes" should be checked. If the subject is not in a flood hazard area, "No" should be checked. Some areas are not mapped for flood hazard purposes and may be identified in the index of a source map as "non-participating communities." If the subject is located in such an area, "No" is the correct response.

In the spaces provided the appraiser records the FEMA zone, the effective date of the map used to identify the flood zone in which the property is located, and the map number. If the subject is situated in a special flood hazard area, the appraiser should attach a copy of the flood map to the appraisal report and indicate the approximate location of the property site.

| D53 | **Comments** | In this section the appraiser summarizes the site description. The site information specifically requested on the form covers the features most typical of single-family residential sites, but other features that affect the value of the site may be present. It is the appraiser's responsibility to describe all favorable and unfavorable site influences and offer an opinion as to their potential effect on the marketability of the property being appraised. Any external obsolescence must also be addressed as depreciation in Section F68, in the Cost Approach, and in the Location section (H79) of the Sales Comparison Analysis.

If the improvements do not represent a legal, conforming use under the current zoning classification, the appraiser must explain here whether the improvements represent an illegal use or a legal, nonconforming use. The appraiser should discuss the effect that the improvements' noncompliance with zoning regulation will have on the marketability and value of the subject property.

Finally, if the appraiser knows that the subject site or a nearby site has been contaminated by a hazardous substance that may impact its value or create an illegal situation, this information must be acknowledged here and discussed further in Section F69.

E	**Description of Improvements**	An important part of every appraisal is the description of the buildings on the site. The appraiser describes each building's size, design, layout, and construction details, including structural components, materials, and mechanical systems. The appraiser also describes the condition of each building element. The building description provides the basis for comparing the improvements of the subject property with improvements that are typical of the subject market area.

Accurate building descriptions are essential to any valuation assignment. A thorough understanding of the physical characteristics of the subject property facilitates the selection of suitable comparables. Building descriptions also provide useful data for identifying the extent and quality of building improvements, calculating their reproduction or replacement costs, and determining various forms of depreciation.

The information required to complete the Uniform Residential Appraisal Report form is specific and designed to provide as detailed a description of the improvements as possible. Any additional explanation should be presented in the comments in Sections F67, F68, and F69 or in an addendum. In this section, as in other sections of the report, the appraiser should be careful to correlate the information reported with the data presented in the valuation sections of the report.

E54	**General Description**	**Number of Units**. The number of units in the dwelling being appraised should be recorded. The entry will usually be "1" because a special appraisal form is normally required for multi-unit buildings. However, a different entry might be appropriate when an "in-law unit" has been added to a single-family residence, or when a duplex has been converted to single-family use.

In instances in which the appraisal of a single-family residence includes more than one unit, the appraiser must consider market acceptability, legal issues, and highest and best use before determining whether the Uniform Residential Appraisal Report form is the appropriate form for reporting the appraisal.

No. of Stories. The number of above-grade levels of finished living space should be entered. The number shown here should also be used to calculate the gross living area in the room list section (E59) and in the Cost Approach section on page two.

Type (Det./Att.). Here the subject property is further described as either "detached" or "attached" to another structure. "Detached" means the subject is separate and freestanding, while "attached" indicates that the subject shares at least one common wall with an adjacent structure.

Design (Style). In this space the appraiser should identify the type of architecture and design, using terminology appropriate to the market area in which the subject property is located. Architectural style may impact the value of the subject and should be considered in the selection and analysis of comparable sales.

Existing/Proposed. If the subject improvements are completed and available for occupancy as of the effective date of appraisal, "Existing" should be entered. If "Proposed" is entered, information on scheduled completion dates and other development-related details should be

Figure 7. Description of Improvements, Section E

DESCRIPTION OF IMPROVEMENTS

GENERAL DESCRIPTION E54
- No. of Units
- No. of Stories
- Type (Det./Att.)
- Design (Style)
- Existing/Proposed
- Age (Yrs.)
- Effective Age (Yrs.)

EXTERIOR DESCRIPTION E55
- Foundation
- Exterior Walls
- Roof Surface
- Gutters & Dwnspts.
- Window Type
- Storm/Screens
- Manufactured House

FOUNDATION E56
- Slab
- Crawl Space
- Basement
- Sump Pump
- Dampness
- Settlement
- Infestation

BASEMENT E57
- Area Sq. Ft.
- % Finished
- Ceiling
- Walls
- Floor
- Outside Entry

INSULATION E58
- Roof ☐
- Ceiling ☐
- Walls ☐
- Floor ☐
- None ☐
- Unknown ☐

ROOMS	Foyer	Living	Dining	Kitchen	Den	Family Rm.	Rec. Rm.	Bedrooms	# Baths	Laundry	Other	Area Sq. Ft.
Basement **E59**												
Level 1												
Level 2												

Finished area **above** grade contains: Rooms;   Bedroom(s);   Bath(s);   Square Feet of Gross Living Area

INTERIOR E60 Materials/Condition
- Floors
- Walls
- Trim/Finish
- Bath Floor
- Bath Wainscot
- Doors

HEATING E61
- Type
- Fuel
- Condition

COOLING E62
- Central
- Other
- Condition

KITCHEN EQUIP.
- Refrigerator ☐
- Range/Oven ☐
- Disposal **E63** ☐
- Dishwasher ☐
- Fan/Hood ☐
- Microwave ☐
- Washer/Dryer ☐

ATTIC E64
- None ☐
- Stairs ☐
- Drop Stair ☐
- Scuttle ☐
- Floor ☐
- Heated ☐
- Finished ☐

AMENITIES E65
- Fireplace(s) # ☐
- Patio ☐
- Deck ☐
- Porch ☐
- Fence ☐
- Pool ☐

CAR STORAGE E66
- None ☐
- Garage ☐   # of cars
- Attached ☐
- Detached ☐
- Built-In ☐
- Carport ☐
- Driveway ☐

provided. Data taken from plans and specifications should be carefully correlated to entries made in the final reconciliation on page two, which will stipulate that the appraisal is made "subject to completion per plans and specifications."

Age (Yrs.). The actual age of the subject improvements in years as of the effective date of valuation should be recorded. This is sometimes referred to as historical or chronological age.

Effective Age (Yrs.). This entry is based on the professional judgment of the appraiser and may be expressed as a precise number or a range. Effective age is the age indicated by the condition and utility of a structure. The effective age of an improvement may be less than its actual age if the building has had better-than-average maintenance, if it is of better quality or design, or if there is an undersupply of such buildings on the market.

The relationship between the actual age and the effective age of the property is a valid indication of its condition. A property that has been well-maintained and modernized when necessary will generally have an effective age that is somewhat lower than its actual age. On the other hand, a property that has not been well-maintained or has physical problems will often have an effective age that is higher than its chronological age.

The effective age recorded here must be correlated to the information presented in the cost approach. When the "estimated remaining economic life" figure entered in Section G71 of the cost approach is added to the estimated effective age, the resultant figure must equal the total estimated economic life of the property that the appraiser applies to calculate physical incurable depreciation in the cost approach.

E55   **Exterior Description**

This entry describes the structural character of the improvements. The appraiser specifies the materials used for the exterior of the structure.

Appraisal Note

The structural frames of most houses in the United States, including many with brick-veneer siding, are made of wood. The three most common types of wooden frame construction are platform, balloon, and post-and-beam. Of the three, platform framing is the most common.

In platform construction, one story of a building is constructed at a time and each story serves as a platform for the next. Studs are cut at the ceiling height of the first story, horizontal plates are than laid on top, and more studs are cut for the second story.

In balloon framing, which is found in older, multistory brick buildings, long studs run from the top of the foundation wall to the roof. They are notched to receive a horizontal framing member at each upper floor level. Balloon framing is rarely used today because the long studs that are needed cost a great deal and this type of framing has poor fire resistance.

Post-and-beam framing is characterized by beams that are spaced up to eight feet apart and are supported on posts and exterior walls. The framing members are much larger and heavier than those used in other framing systems. The post-and-beam system was used in colonial houses and barns and regained popularity beginning in the mid-1970s.

One relatively recent method of framing employs panels of framing members and siding or subflooring that are prefabricated at a mill or built on site. Construction begins on the ground and materials to be added later are lifted as a unit and installed in place. Some buildings are constructed with solid masonry exterior walls which act as part of the framing system. Often interior framing is constructed of steel beams or reinforced concrete. Older masonry buildings have interior framing made of wooden beams and posts.

**Exterior
Description
(continued)**

The URAR form lists the components most important to the exterior description of residential improvements. On each line the appraiser enters the type of material used for that component.

Foundation. The appraiser should record the type of foundation materials used, such as poured concrete or cinder block walls. Many older foundations are made of cut stone or stone and brick. In all cases the type of material used should be specified.

Exterior Walls. The appraiser should specify the primary material used for the exterior wall covering—e.g., wood siding (clapboard, board and batten), wood or asbestos shingles, stucco, or brick. A brick exterior should be further described as either veneer (brick on some form of masonry block) or solid masonry.

Roof Surface. The appraiser identifies the material used for roof covering. In most regions of the United States, asphalt shingles are typically used for residential roofing. Other common residential roofing materials are shingles and shakes made of wood (usually cedar), asbestos, and cement. Fiberglass shingles have recently been introduced, and metal, clay tiles, slate, and built-up or membrane roofs are also used in some areas.

Gutters and Downspouts. The material used for gutters and downspouts should be specified. If these features are not present, the appraiser should state this fact and, in the comments section or an addendum, note the width of the roof's overhand and the site grading around the foundation walls. Any evidence of dampness in the basement, craw space, or slab should also be noted to indicate the potential for damage due to rainfall.

Window Type. The appraiser describes the major type of windows used in the subject property. Window types include single- and double-hung, casement, horizontal sliding, clerestory, fixed, awning, hopper, center pivot, and jalousie. Wood was the material first used for window frames and is still the most common material found in houses.

Wood provides good insulation, is readily available, takes a natural or painted finish, and is easy to install and repair. Windows may also have aluminum or steel frames. An appropriate entry here might be "aluminum casement" or "wood jalousie."

Storm/Screens. The presence of storm windows may be important to the value estimate. Because storm windows provide good insulation, they are fuel-efficient and can provide substantial energy cost savings. Wooden storm windows that are removed and stored during the summer are becoming obsolete. Most modern storm windows are made of aluminum and are permanently installed. Appraisers may find it difficult to determine how much storm windows add to a property's value in certain residential markets. An indication may be derived, however, by analyzing what is typical and expected in the neighborhood. In most parts of the country, screens are needed for all windows that open. Older screens may have wood frames, but mesh screens with aluminum frames are now more common. In many residential properties, screens are combined with storm windows. The appraiser should identify the type of storm windows and screens provided and note whether any are missing.

Manufactured House. The appraiser should state whether the subject improvements are manufactured housing. If this is the case, a more detailed description of the quality, character, compatibility, and marketability of the structure will be necessary. Prefabricated and modular houses are manufactured and partially constructed before they are positioned on their sites. Most lenders have eligibility criteria for mortgages secured by manufactured housing. The appraiser should become familiar with the Department of Housing and Urban Development's manufactured housing construction and safety standards and with the specific requirements of the client before appraising this type of property. In selecting comparable sales properties for the appraisal of a manufactured house, the appraiser should use sales of other manufactured homes or conventionally built homes that have been adjusted for differences in quality and marketability.

E56	Foundation	Further information on the type of foundation and a description of the basement are included in this section. A "Yes" or "No" entry may be entered on the lines provided next to "Slab," "Crawl Space," and "Basement." If there is no evidence of dampness, settlement, or infestation, a comment such as "None" or "None observed" is entered on these lines. If there is evidence of dampness, settlement, or infestation, the appraiser must note the location and general extent of the problem on the appropriate line. These conditions are to be discussed further in the comments entered in Section F68, in the Cost Approach in Section G, in the Sales Comparison Analysis in Section H, and in the comments and conditions of the appraisal in Section J. The appraiser may also recommend a thorough inspection by a qualified professional.

E57	Basement	On the Uniform Residential Appraisal Report form, basement space is considered separately from gross living area and the room count. Any finished area in the basement should be fully described in Section F67.

Area Sq. Ft. The gross basement area should be calculated and noted here. "N/A" is entered if no basement exists.

% Finished. The amount of finished area should be estimated and recorded. This percentage is calculated by dividing the indicated square footage of basement area by the ground floor living area, i.e., the building's "footprint." The percent of finished basement area and the basement area shown in the room list (Section E59) should be clearly stated in Section F67 and be consistent with the square footage allocations used in the approaches to value. "Unfinished" is the appropriate entry if the foundation, wall studs, and floor joists are exposed.

Additional information is required to describe the materials used to finish basement ceilings, walls, and floors. If outside entry or access is available, it should be noted and described.

Insulation   During the physical inspection of the improvements, the appraiser should note the existence, location, and R value of the insulation. Supplemental information can be obtained from the home owner, from the owner's agent, or from construction plans, if available. The appraiser should check for insulation in the roof, ceiling, walls, and floors and mark the appropriate box for each place insulation is found. If the R values are known, they are entered in the spaces provided; otherwise "Unknown" is the appropriate entry. "None" is checked if the structure is not insulated and "Unknown" is checked if it cannot be determined whether or not the improvements are insulated.

The overall contribution of insulation to the property's market value should be considered in Section F67, in the Cost Approach in Section G, in the Sales Comparison Analysis in Section H, and in Reconciliation, Section J.

There is no universal standard for the amount of insulation a structure should have. The amount needed varies with the climate and the type of building. For example, overceiling or underroof insulation with an R value of 13 might be satisfactory in a mild climate if the building has gas or oil heat and no air-conditioning. In colder or hotter climates, and in residences with electric heat or air-conditioning, insulation with an R value of 24 might be necessary.

Appraisal Note   The ability of insulating materials to resist the flow of heat is measured in R values. An R value is derived by measuring the British thermal units (Btus) that are transmitted through one thickness of the insulation in one hour. The higher the R value, the more effective the insulation.

Insulation materials and methods of application vary. Loosefill insulations are poured or machine-blown into place and are composed primarily of mineral wool or cellulose fiber. Flexible insulation is also made of mineral wool or cellulose fiber, but it is produced in the form of blankets or batts. The batts may be covered on one or both sides with kraft paper or foil, which serves as a vapor barrier. Rigid insulation is found in newer structures and comes in four forms: structural wall insulation, fiberboard, structural deck insulation, and rigid board insulation. Reflective insulation is made of metallic foil and reflects heat transferred by radiation. Foamed-in-place insulation is available in two types: urethane foam and urea-formaldehyde foam. After it is in place, foam insulation chemically expands to approximately 30 times its original size and then solidifies.

Two types of insulation are potentially hazardous to human health: asbestos and urea-formaldehyde foam. Asbestos is a nonflammable, fibrous material that was used in construction between 1945 and 1970; urea-formaldehyde foam was used during the 1960s and 1970s. If the appraiser knows that either of these substances is present in or near the subject property, it is imperative that this fact be disclosed in Section F69 or in an addendum to the report. The appraiser must also recognize any effect on the market value of the building created by the current or past presence of asbestos or urea-formaldehyde foam insulation, and address this factor in the comments and conditions of the Reconciliation (Section J).

E59   **Room List**

In this part of the report the appraiser provides a record of all the rooms contained within the subject structure and identifies those included in the total room count.

The columns in the upper half of this section list the room types most frequently found in single-family residences. In the blanks provided, the appraiser enters the number of rooms of each type found on each level of the subject property. Rooms that are not specifically listed on the form, such as a breakfast room or solarium, are entered by name on the appropriate line in the "Other" column. Some homes contain a level not shown on the form such as a third story or an above-ground, lower living level, which is typical of hillside homes. The appraiser may use the blank space at the bottom of the room list to insert a living level not listed on the form and then enter the number of rooms of each type. The rooms listed here and their locations must correspond to those identified in the building sketch.

In the "Area Sq. Ft." column, the appraiser records the total square footage on each level, including the basement. These figures should match those previously calculated from the external measurements taken during the inspection and must correspond to those that appear on the building sketch.

The last space in Section E59 asks for information on the "Finished Area Above Grade." Local practice generally determines the portion of a residence that qualifies as a basement, although basement area is typically below grade. In this section of the form, basement rooms—whether finished or unfinished, below or above grade—are reflected in the "Basement" section (E57), but are not included in the calculation of above-grade gross living area.

In the first space, marked "Rooms," the appraiser enters the total number of rooms above grade. This should be the same figure used in the Sales Comparison Analysis, but may differ from the total number of rooms identified in the preceding grid for three reasons:

1. In most areas it is normal practice to exclude foyers, baths, attics, porches, sleeping lofts, breezeways, and laundry rooms from the room count.
2. The treatment of dining areas, dinettes, retreats, and other room areas in open floor plans varies from region to region.
3. Basement and attic rooms are excluded from the total number of rooms above grade.

The appraiser should be familiar with and use local methods of determining room count.

In the second space, the appraiser records the number of bedrooms. This figure should correspond to the number of bedrooms listed in the preceding grid, the figure used in the Sales Comparison Analysis section, and the total number of bedrooms shown in the building sketch. A bedroom typically has at least one built-in closet. Bedrooms are usually included in the total room count and also listed separately.

In the next space, the appraiser enters the bathroom count. This figure should correspond with the total number of baths listed in the preceding section, the figure used in the Sales Comparison Analysis section, and the total number shown in the building sketch. Typically, three or more plumbing fixtures (wash basin, toilet, and tub or shower) constitute a bath; two fixtures (wash basin and toilet) comprise a half-bath. A single plumbing fixture is not considered a portion of a bath. Bathrooms are typically excluded from the total room count.

In the last space, the appraiser enters the total square feet of gross living area. This figure is derived from the external measurements taken at the time of inspection and should correspond to the sum of the "Area Sq. Ft." figures shown in the grid (excluding the basement), the total above-grade living area calculations shown in the building sketch, the total above-grade square footage used in the Cost Approach section, and the gross living area figure employed in the Sales Comparison Analysis section.

The importance of correlating the room list and the corresponding information in the Sales Comparison Analysis section cannot be overemphasized. Because room count is calculated in different ways, the appraiser must be careful to ensure consistency between the subject and the comparable sales analyzed.

Appraisal Note

In reporting room count, certain principles are commonly applied to combination rooms. These principles are based on room size and market acceptance. Living room-dining room combinations and kitchen-dining room combinations represent the most common examples. In most markets these combined areas are counted as one room unless they are so large that they could be partitioned into two separate rooms that meet neighborhood standards.

Again, the appraiser must be consistent and apply the same method of counting rooms to the subject and to each comparable property.

E60

Interior

Since interior surface materials and condition may vary from room to room, entries in this section should describe the most prevalent type and condition of surface materials used throughout the interior of the house. There should be consistency between the information reported here and in the comments in Section F68, in the Cost Approach (Section G70), and in Section H86 of the Sales Comparison Analysis grid.

Floors. The appraiser should describe the floor finish in the major sectors of the house. Wood in various forms continues to be a common flooring material, but other types of flooring have also become popular. A wide variety of resilient, ceramic, and quarry tiles are used in residential construction. Resilient flooring, usually composed of a combination of vinyl and asphalt, is also widely used. Carpeting, once considered a luxury, is now common in residences. The appraiser must consider how floor coverings will stand up to daily use and how they are incorporated into the building design and decor.

Walls. This section describes the most common types of wall finish found throughout the house. In residences, most interior walls are made of wall studs covered with materials such as gypsum board, wood paneling, ceramic tile, plywood, and hardboard. Plaster was once popular, but is used less frequently today. The wall material most widely used in interior residential construction is drywall, which is also called plaster board, Sheetrock, or gypsum board. Masonry houses often have masonry interior walls. Glass, wood, plywood, hardboard, metals, tiles, concrete, brick, and a number of other products are used in wall construction. Interior house walls are usually painted, wallpapered, or covered with decorative products.

Trim/Finish. The appearance of moldings and baseboards is considered here as well as the quality of interior painting and decorating. In the past architects often designed unique moldings for buildings, and beautiful, restored moldings add value to older houses. Today moldings are of a standard size and shape, and their use is decreasing. Simple baseboards are widely used to protect walls from damage by cleaning equipment and furniture.

What constitutes attractive painting and decoration is subjective. Most new owners and tenants redecorate to suit their personal tastes. Nevertheless, unusual decorations and colors may have limited appeal and can detract from a home's marketability.

Bath Floor. The most common type of bathroom flooring found in the subject property should be recorded here. Ceramic tile and vinyl materials continue to be used most frequently, but other materials such as hardwood, carpeting, and marble are also popular. As with the flooring in other parts of the residence, the appraiser must evaluate the condition of the flooring and determine how well it conforms to the home's design and overall finish.

Bath Wainscot. The appraiser indicates the most common type of material used on shower walls and around tubs and wash basins. Ceramic tile, Formica, fiberglass, and other synthetic, water-resistant materials are popular.

Doors. Here the appraiser describes the type of doors found in the subject. Exterior doors are typically made of solid wood, metal, or glass. Any special type of door construction must be described by the appraiser. The presence or absence of energy-conserving materials such as weatherstripping around doors should also be noted. Air leakage through cracks at the bottom of doors can be stopped with door shoes, weatherproof thresholds, and sweeps. Interior, hollow-core wood doors, which are considered real property, are used in most residential construction.

E61   **Heating**   Here the appraiser identifies the type, fuel, and condition of the subject's heating system. The type most often will be forced air, gravity air, or electric fueled by oil, coal, wood, or liquid gas. Conclusions concerning the condition of the heating system should be based on the appraiser's observations. If the heating system is deficient or does not meet market expectations, the appraiser must discuss its potential effect on the overall condition and appeal of the property in the comments in Section F68. If physical or functional depreciation is attributed to a deficiency in the heating system, the Sales Comparison Analysis should also reflect this fact in Sections H86 and/or H90.

| E62 | Cooling |

To indicate whether the property is improved with a central cooling system, the appraiser enters "Yes" or "No" in the space provided. If cooling is provided by other means, these means should be specified. Portable and window air conditioners are considered personal property, even if they are provided by a landlord, and are excluded from the valuation of the property. On the other hand, a central cooling system built into the structure is valued as part of the real property. If the subject improvements lack a cooling system, "None" is the appropriate entry. Where more than one type of cooling system is used, the appraiser should note the predominant method and provide further details in Section F68. Conclusions pertaining to the subject's cooling system should be based on research and observation and should reflect existing market expectations.

| E63 | Kitchen Equipment |

This section lists the equipment most commonly found in the kitchens of single-family residences. By checking the appropriate box, the appraiser verifies that, as of the date of the inspection, the designated fixture is "in place" and is an operating item of real property. Equipment that is personal property is identified with the letter "P" on the form and not considered in the valuation process.

The kitchen is a very important component of any residential property. In single-family homes, the kitchen costs more to construct and usually serves more functions than any other room in the house. A well-designed and well-maintained kitchen may add substantial value to a property, while a poorly designed or poorly maintained kitchen can substantially decrease a property's market appeal.

Although kitchen appliances are generally treated as short-lived items, they are relatively expensive to replace. The appraiser should be prepared to analyze the quality, quantity, and condition of the appliances installed in the subject in relation to those found in competing properties. Their effect on value should be addressed in the comments in Section F68, in the depreciation analysis in the Cost Approach (Section G), and in Section H86 of the Sales Comparison Analysis grid.

| E64 | Attic |

The attic of a residence is generally located between the rafters and the ceiling joists. If the property has an attic, the appraiser checks the appropriate box to specify the type of access. "Stairs" refers to permanent stairs leading to the attic entrance. "Drop stairs" are affixed to the ceiling or wall and must be pulled down or unfolded to be used. A "scuttle" is a covered hatch in the ceiling, usually located in a closet or hallway, that provides entry to the attic. If the attic has a floor or is heated or finished, the appraiser checks the appropriate boxes.

Typically attics are not included in the above-grade living area. However, the appraiser must make this determination based on the attic's finish, heating and cooling system, ceiling height, type of access, and local building code regulations. Attic space judged to be above-grade living area should not be described in this section; rather, it should be included in the room list (E59). Attics that have functional utility may be an attractive feature, warranting their inclusion in both the Cost Approach and Sales Comparison Analysis sections of the form.

Amenities In this section of the report the appraiser identifies the amenities that are part of the subject property. When amenities are present, they may contribute value to the property and should be specifically analyzed and addressed in the valuation sections of the appraisal report. The amenity items listed in this section, fireplace, patio, deck, porch, fence, and pool, are those most commonly found in residential properties. Space is also provided to identify an additional amenity.

The appraiser is responsible for identifying all amenities within the subject improvements or on the subject site that contribute value to the property. The dimensions of porches, patios, and decks should be recorded here or on the floor plan sketch that is attached to the report. Any additional information describing these features should be provided in Section F67. Any comments concerning the presence or condition of amenities should be made in Section F68 and discussed further in the Cost Approach (Section G). The appraiser must correlate the amenities described here with the information presented in the Sales Comparison Analysis, Sections H86, H93, H94, and, if appropriate, H98.

Fireplace(s) #. The type and number of fireplaces should be recorded in the designated space. Most fireplaces are of masonry such as stone or brick and have a single opening with a damper and a hearth. If the fireplace is of the metal, freestanding type, this should be noted.

Usually fireplaces are not the building's primary source of heat. In fact, because of their design, many have little heating power. Because fireplaces are difficult to construct, many are not well-made and function poorly. One common problem is downdraft, whereby smoke is blown into the house when it is windy outside. This can happen frequently if the stack does not extend at least two feet above any part of the roof within ten feet of the chimney.

Many prefabricated fireplaces and flues are installed in homes that previously did not have fireplaces. Unless they are approved by Underwriters Laboratories and installed according to the manufacturer's instructions, they can be a potential fire hazard. To be safe, a fireplace should be supported by noncombustible material and have a noncombustible hearth extending at least 16 inches in front of the opening and at least eight inches on each side. Carpeting placed near a fireplace opening is a potential fire hazard.

Patio. Most patios are designed for outdoor use in a private, protected area of the property with access to the house. If the subject property has one or more patios, the prevalent material used such as "brick" or "concrete," is recorded. "None" is the appropriate entry if the subject does not have a patio.

Deck. Most decks are constructed of wood and are either attached or freestanding. They are usually situated where there are access doors from the dwelling, at ground level or above. In recent years some home owners have begun constructing decks farther from the house to serve as platforms for hot tubs or as outdoor garden seating areas. If the subject property is improved with a deck or decks, the box is checked and the material used is noted. "None" is entered if there is no deck.

Porch. Porches are generally constructed over a foundation. When located at the front of the home, a porch usually provides a focal point for the entry as well as protection from the elements. Porches constructed at the side or rear of a house are normally used for outdoor living and designed for a certain amount of privacy. Porches may be described as open, covered, enclosed, or screened. The box is checked if a porch exists and the type of porch is entered in the space. "None" is entered if there is no porch.

Fence. Fences and walls screen or enclose portions of a site. They can provide varying degrees of privacy, security, and attractiveness to the property and may be constructed of a variety of materials, including wood, metal, concrete, and stone. Some type of perimeter fencing between properties is common in many areas of the country. Appraisers should determine whether perimeter fencing is part of the subject property or an adjacent site. If the subject's fencing encroaches on an adjoining site, or if an adjoining site's fencing encroaches on the subject site, this fact should be noted and its potential effect on value reported.

Pool. In this entry the appraiser reports the existence of a permanently installed swimming pool. Pools vary in type, size, and quality. A pool's contribution to the value of a single-family residence also varies from region to region and neighborhood to neighborhood. If the subject site is improved with a pool, the appraiser should check the appropriate box and identify the type of pool such as "in-ground Gunite" or "above-ground liner." The appraiser should also discuss the age and condition of the pool in the comments in Sections F67 and F68, in the Cost Approach (Section G), and in Section H93 and possibly H98 of the Sales Comparison Analysis.

E66   **Car Storage**

In this section the appraiser describes the type of car storage provided. If there is no facility for auto storage or off-street parking, the box opposite "None" is checked. If the improvement provided is a garage, the number of cars accommodated is entered opposite the garage type, "Attached," "Detached," or "Built-in." "Attached" indicates that the garage shares at least a portion of a common wall with the house. "Detached" indicates that the garage is a separate structure. "Built-in" describes a garage that has more than one wall in common with the house and has a living area above or around it.

If the subject is improved with a carport, the appraiser enters the number of cars that can be accommodated on the appropriate line. The "Driveway" line is used to indicate that an open, off-street parking area exists, and the number of autos it can accommodate with adequate space for ingress and egress is recorded.

The appraiser determines whether the car storage is adequate or inadequate based on neighborhood norms for homes similar to the subject. If the storage is inadequate, an explanation should be provided in Section F68. The appraiser may also need to assign functional obsolescence for this deficiency in the Cost Approach and the Sales Comparison Analysis sections.

F	**Comments**	In this space the appraiser provides information on any physical items not previously described and offers additional explanations. Key conclusions to be considered in the valuation sections of the report are summarized.
F67	**Additional features (special energy efficient items, etc.)**	Here the appraiser discusses special energy-efficient items that are included in or absent from the subject property. These items might include solar hot water heaters, auto setback thermostats, and double- or triple-glazed windows. Also discussed are special interior features such as skylights, wet bars, and unique finishes. Other items previously noted but requiring additional description here might include site improvements such as landscaping, pools, and outbuildings.
F68	**Condition of the improvements, depreciation (physical, functional and external), repairs needed, etc.**	In this section the appraiser comments on any items of physical, functional, or external depreciation to be considered in the valuation sections of the report. Depreciation could be attributed to the condition of the foundation, siding and roofing, interior floors, kitchen equipment, and electrical system or to any room additions and conversions.
F69	**Adverse environmental conditions (such as, but not limited to, hazardous wastes, toxic substances, etc.) present in the improvements, on the site, or In the immediate vicinity of the subject property**	All environmental conditions that are observed or otherwise known to the appraiser which could impact either the subject neighborhood or subject property values must be disclosed. These may include geological hazards such as flood, mudslide, or earthquake zones and toxic hazards such as radon, asbestos, urea-formaldehyde insulation, and chemical pollutants in the air or groundwater.
	Standards Note	Guide Note 8 to the Standards of Professional Appraisal Practice of the Appraisal Institute addresses the subject of hazardous substances. It stipulates: *The appraiser should note in the report any condition that is observed during the inspection of the subject property or becomes known to the appraiser through the normal research involved in performing the appraisal which would lead the appraiser to believe that hazardous substances may be present in or on the subject property, or is at variance with information or descriptions provided by others.*
	Fannie Mae Note	When the appraiser has knowledge of an environmental hazard (whether it exists in or on the subject property or on a site within the vicinity of the property), he or she must note the hazardous condition in the appraisal report. The appraiser must also comment on any influence the hazard has on the value and marketability of the prop-

Figure 8. Comments, Section F

COMMENTS	
Additional features (special energy efficient items, etc.): **F67**	
Condition of the improvements, depreciation (physical, functional, and external), repairs needed, quality of construction, remodeling/additions, etc.: **F68**	
Adverse environmental conditions (such as, but not limited to, hazardous wastes, toxic substances, etc.) present in the improvements, on the site, or in the immediate vicinity of the subject property: **F69**	

46

erty (if it is measurable through an analysis of comparable market data as of the effective date of the appraisal) and make appropriate adjustments in the overall analysis of the property's value.

Fannie Mae does not consider the appraiser to be an expert in the field of environmental hazards. The typical residential real estate appraiser is neither expected nor required to be an expert in this specialized field. However, he or she does have a responsibility to note in the appraisal report any adverse conditions that were observed during the inspection of the subject property and any information that he or she has become aware of through the normal research involved in performing an appraisal. (See Freddie Mac Form 439/Fannie Mae Form 1004B, Revised 6/93, Statement of Limiting Conditions and Appraiser's Certification.)

Figure 9. Cost Approach, Section G

COST APPROACH

ESTIMATED SITE VALUE . . . . = $ _____

ESTIMATED REPRODUCTION COST-NEW OF IMPROVEMENTS:

Dwelling _____ Sq. Ft. @ $ _____ = $ _____

_____ Sq. Ft. @ $ _____ = _____

= _____

Garage/Carport _____ Sq. Ft. @ $ _____ = _____

Total Estimated Cost New . . . . = $ _____

Less Physical | Functional | External

Depreciation _____ = $ _____

Depreciated Value of Improvements . . . . = $ _____

"As-is" Value of Site Improvements . . . . = $ _____

INDICATED VALUE BY COST APPROACH . . . . = $ _____

`G70`

Comments on Cost Approach (such as, source of cost estimate, site value, square foot calculation and, for HUD, VA, and FmHA, the estimated remaining economic life of the property): _____ `G71`

_____

_____

_____

_____

_____

_____

Page Two of the URAR Form

Once all the factual information about the subject property has been gathered and recorded and some general comparisons have been made between the subject and other properties, the appraiser is ready to begin estimating the market value of the subject property. The second page of the Uniform Residential Appraisal Report form has sections on all three approaches to value and a section for reconciliation of the value indications derived.

Usually the income approach is only applicable to residential properties located in neighborhoods with a heavy concentration of rental properties. For properties located in areas where most residences are owner-occupied, the income approach is usually not a reliable valuation technique.

The appraiser should make certain that the figures recorded on page two of the form correspond with those entered on page one.

G

Cost Approach

The cost approach is useful in the valuation of residential properties because it reflects the concerns of buyers in the market. Many market participants equate value with cost, so the cost of constructing a building with the same functional utility as the subject property less depreciation may be a valid measure of the subject's value. Another benefit of applying the cost approach is the identification and quantification of the accrued depreciation in the property.

The cost approach is most valid in the appraisal of new or nearly new residential construction. If improvements are new, it can be assumed that the property is being employed at its highest and best use or something very close to it, and only minor adjustments need to be made for depreciation. If the improvements are older, however, depreciation is more difficult to estimate and there is a greater chance that the property's current use is not the highest and best use.

In the development of the cost approach, Fannie Mae and Freddie Mac require that the appraiser provide:

1. Square foot building calculations, i.e., the mathematics that result in the square footage estimate used in the Cost Approach section. The total gross living area calculated must be consistent with the figures entered in the room list (E59), the "Dwelling" lines under "Estimated Reproduction Cost - New of Improvements" in Section G70, and the "Price/Gross Living Area" section (H75) in the Sales Comparison Analysis.

2. Comments on the cost approach. The appraiser must address all physical deficiencies. If any of these deficiencies affect the health and safety of the property's occupants, the problem must be corrected or the mortgage secured by the subject property will not be eligible for purchase. An addendum may be necessary if this section and Section F68 do not provide sufficient space for complete discussion of the property's inadequacies.

Estimated site value. The value of a site is usually estimated by comparing sales of similar land parcels transferred at approximately the same time as the effective date of appraisal. The comparable sites should have characteristics similar to those of the subject parcel to make a valid comparison. To apply this method the appraiser gathers and analyzes information on sale prices, dates of sale, financing and terms of sale, parcel size, location, physical site characteristics, and other value-influencing factors.

A sales comparison analysis for estimating land value is similar to the sales comparison approach applied to estimate improved property value. The four steps of the procedure are listed below.

1. Collect data on sales of similar properties as well as ground leases, listings, offers, and renewal options.
2. Analyze the data for comparability with the subject site. This is accomplished by developing appropriate units of comparison and applying these units to each element of comparison.
3. Adjust the sale prices of the comparable parcels to reflect any differences between these parcels and the subject.
4. Reconcile the results into a single value indication or range of values for the subject site.

Regardless of the method used, the site value must be based on relevant, documented market evidence. The criteria for site valuation should be explained in the comments in Section G71. When necessary, a sales comparison spreadsheet or another suitable addendum should be attached.

Estimated reproduction cost new of improvements. After the appraiser has inspected the subject property and gathered all relevant data pertaining to the neighborhood, the site, and the improvements, certain steps must be taken to derive a value indication by the cost approach. The steps in the cost approach as outlined on the appraisal form are

1. Estimate the replacement or reproduction cost new of the structure as of the effective date of the appraisal. Total cost new includes all extras, energy-efficient items, porches, and garages or carports.
2. Estimate the amount of accrued depreciation categorized as physical deterioration, functional obsolescence, and external obsolescence.
3. Deduct accrued depreciation from total cost new to derive the depreciated value of the improvements.
4. Add the depreciated cost of building improvements to the "as is" value of the site improvements to obtain the indicated total value of the subject property.

Reproduction cost is the cost of constructing a precise duplicate or exact replica of the structure being appraised, using the same construction and design standards and embodying all inherent structural deficiencies, superadequacies, and items of obsolescence. *Replacement cost* is the cost of constructing a structure with utility equivalent to the subject improvements with modern materials and according to current design standards. Replacement cost estimates are often used when estimating reproduction cost is impractical due to the age of the structure or the difficulty of estimating the actual cost to duplicate a building constructed with an unusual design or outdated materials.

Although estimating reproduction cost new as of the date of appraisal is sometimes difficult, the procedure provides a basis for measuring all types of depreciation. The use of replacement cost eliminates the need to estimate some forms of functional obsolescence, but other forms of functional obsolescence, physical deterioration, and external obsolescence must still be estimated.

Dwelling area calculations. To complete this entry the appraiser records the total gross living area based on exterior measurements. This figure should be consistent with the information presented in the exterior building sketch. Dwelling area includes finished, habitable above-grade living area only. Finished basement or attic space is calculated and shown in the extra space. The appraiser may record the square foot calculation for the structure in this space or may indicate it on the exterior building sketch, which Fannie Mae requires as an exhibit in the addenda to each appraisal report.

Square-foot cost. The appraiser estimates improvement cost by comparing the subject property in terms of dollars per square foot of gross building area with similar structures recently completed or under construction for which cost information is available. The estimate may be derived using data on actual construction costs for houses located in the subject area or data from recognized cost reporting services. Most cost manuals provide cost figures on prototype structures and indicate adjustments that can be made to the base data to reflect the physical and locational features of the subject property more closely.

Square-foot costs vary with building size. When a standard construction cost is allocated over a larger area, the unit cost is less. This principle is reflected by the fact that bathrooms, kitchens, plumbing, and heating units do not cost proportionately more in a larger home than in a smaller one.

On the first line next to "Dwelling," the appraiser estimates the square foot area and cost of the first and second stories of the house. This is considered the primary living area. The next line may be used to record the square foot area and related cost of finished basement or attic space. On the third line the appraiser furnishes cost information relating to special features and extra value items.

Garage/carport and total cost. The gross area and allocated cost per square foot of the garage or carport should be calculated and entered in the space provided. Finally, all the itemized cost components are added together to arrive at the "Total Estimated Cost New."

Less depreciation. The depreciation estimate must be supported with calculations and consistent with the comments presented in previous sections of the report. The depreciation estimated should be allocated to one or more of the three categories listed: physical, functional, and external.

Depreciation is defined as a loss in value from any cause. Deterioration, or physical depreciation, is evidenced by wear and tear, decay, dry rot, cracks, encrustation, or structural defects. Other types of depreciation are caused by obsolescence, which can be either functional or external. Functional obsolescence may result from inadequacy or superadequacy in size, style, or mechanical equipment. Physical deterioration and functional obsolescence are inherent in the improvement itself. External obsolescence is caused by conditions outside the subject property such as changes in demand, property uses in the subject area, zoning, financing, and federal regulations—i.e., economic and locational conditions.

Accrued depreciation is the difference between an improvement's reproduction or replacement cost new and its market value as of the date of appraisal. Several methods may be used to estimate accrued depreciation. Each is acceptable, provided that it is applied consistently and logically and reflects how an informed, prudent buyer would react to the conditions encountered in the structure being appraised. To derive an accurate, supportable estimate of accrued depreciation by any method, the appraiser must consider all property elements that may cause a diminution in value and measures each element only once. Regardless of the method or combination of methods employed, the depreciation estimate must correspond with the information provided on the front of the form and summarized in the Sections F68 and F69.

Depreciated value of improvements. To determine the depreciated value of the improvements, the appraiser subtracts the total depreciation from all causes from the total estimated cost new figure. The result is entered on the space provided.

"As is " value of site improvements. The placement of this entry on the form and the "as is" notation indicate that an estimate of the site improvement value, not cost, is required. Site improvements include driveways, patios, retaining walls, fencing, and landscaping, and their value is usually estimated as a lump sum based on the total contribution of these items to the overall value of the property. The value contribution reflects what the market will pay, i.e., how much the sale price is increased by the inclusion of these specific items.

Indicated value by cost approach. On this line the appraiser totals the dollar amounts of the estimated site value, the depreciated value of the structure, and the "as is" value of the site improvements. This total is the indicated value by the cost approach.

G71 **Comments on Cost Approach (such as, source for cost estimate, site value, square foot calculation and, for HUD, VA and FmHA, the estimated remaining economic life of the property)**

In this section the appraiser supports the assumptions and estimates used in developing the cost approach and provides the source of the data employed. Here the appraiser can identify and describe the source of the cost data, present the square foot building area calculations, and, when applicable, comment on the market trends that influence site value.

A typical entry in this section might read as follows:

> Site value is based on a review of recently consummated comparable land sales. See addendum, Exhibit E, for site valuation

analysis. Cost new estimates are based on information provided by contractor Jack Russell of W.A. Rose Construction Company and confirmed by prototype building cost data published by the XYZ Cost Index. Total accrued depreciation (physical) is estimated by the age-life method using an effective age of five years and a remaining economic life of 45 years.

Appraisal Note

To estimate remaining economic life the appraiser calculates the number of years, as of the date of appraisal, that the property will remain competitive in the open market, i.e., the estimated number of years during which the improvements can be expected to contribute to the value of the property. In this period of time the remaining utility of the structure will be used up. An appraiser derives an estimate of remaining economic life by interpreting the attitudes and behavior of typical buyers of competitive properties. The estimate of remaining economic life should be correlated with projections of total economic life, effective age, estimated depreciation, and assumptions concerning neighborhood trends.

Figure 10. Sales Comparison Analysis, Section H

ITEM	SUBJECT	COMPARABLE NO. 1		COMPARABLE NO. 2		COMPARABLE NO. 3	
Address H72							
Proximity to Subject H73							
Sales Price H74	$	$		$		$	
Price/Gross Liv. Area $ H75 ⊠		$ ⊠		$ ⊠		$ ⊠	
Data and/or H76 Verification Sources							
VALUE ADJUSTMENTS	DESCRIPTION	DESCRIPTION	+(−)$Adjustment	DESCRIPTION	+(−)$Adjustment	DESCRIPTION	+(−)$Adjustment
Sales or Financing Concessions H77							
Date of Sale/Time H78							
Location H79							
Leasehold/Fee Simple H80							
Site H81							
View H82							
Design and Appeal H83							
Quality of Construction H84							
Age H85							
Condition H86							
Above Grade H87 Room Count	Total Bdrms Baths	Total Bdrms Baths		Total Bdrms Baths		Total Bdrms Baths	
Gross Living Area	Sq. Ft.	Sq. Ft.		Sq. Ft.		Sq. Ft.	
Basement & Finished Rooms Below Grade H88							
Functional Utility H89							
Heating/Cooling H90							
Energy Efficient Items H91							
Garage/Carport H92							
Porch, Patio, Deck, Fireplace(s), etc. H93							
Fence, Pool, etc. H94							
H95							
Net Adj. (total) H96		☐ + ☐ − $		☐ + ☐ − $		☐ + ☐ − $	
Adjusted Sales Price of Comparable H97		$		$		$	

Comments on Sales Comparison (including the subject property's compatibility to the neighborhood, etc.): H98

ITEM	SUBJECT	COMPARABLE NO. 1	COMPARABLE NO. 2	COMPARABLE NO. 3
Date, Price and Data Source for prior sales within year of appraisal H99				

Analysis of any current agreement of sale, option, or listing of the subject property and analysis of any prior sales of subject and comparables within one year of the date of appraisal: H100

INDICATED VALUE BY SALES COMPARISON APPROACH . . . . $ H101

SALES COMPARISON ANALYSIS

Sales Comparison Analysis

Analysis of market data is essential to the valuation of single-family residential properties. The sales comparison approach is based on direct comparison of the characteristics of similar residential properties that have recently been sold and transferred in a competitive market. The sales selected as comparables should be demonstrably competitive alternatives to the subject property. Although the Uniform Residential Appraisal Report form provides space for the inclusion of only three comparable sales, the appraiser should include in an addendum any and all sales necessary to support the indicated value estimate.

In the sales comparison approach the appraiser analyzes recent sales of comparable properties located within the subject neighborhood. If the appraiser uses sales of properties located outside the subject neighborhood as comparables, an explanation should be provided.

When appraising a property in a new subdivision or a unit in a new or recently converted condominium, planned unit development, or cooperative project, the appraiser should, if possible, use two comparables from outside the new subdivision or project. Resales from within the subdivision or project are acceptable, however, if they represent arm's-length transactions.

In adjusting for physical differences between properties, comparable sales data should be adjusted *to* the subject property. The subject is the standard against which each comparable sale is evaluated. Thus, if a feature of the comparable property is superior to the same feature in the subject, a minus (-) adjustment to the sale price of the comparable is required to make the comparable equal to the subject property in terms of that feature. Conversely, if an item in the comparable property is inferior to an item in the subject, a plus (+) adjustment is needed to make this component of the comparable equal to the same item in the subject.

Proper appraisal practice requires that adjustments be supported by documented market evidence. In many instances, the most appropriate and generally accepted means of developing a market-based price adjustment is use of the paired data analysis technique. With this procedure an appraiser can derive the amount of value or increment in price attributable to a specific element of comparison. When two comparables are identical or very similar in all but one characteristic, it may be concluded that the difference between them accounts for the difference in their prices. For example, if a property is sold twice within a defined period of time and no changes occur in the property or its environment within that period, an adjustment for market conditions may be calculated from the prices recorded in the two transactions. If two similar properties located in different neighborhoods are sold within a limited time period, an adjustment for location can be derived. In practice, several matched pairs should be isolated from the comparable sales to provide an adequate sampling base for the value conclusion.

The format for reporting sales comparison analysis on the URAR form consists of a grid and comments section, a sales history and comments section, and a line for recording the indicated value of the subject property by the sales comparison approach.

In the first portion of the grid, the appraiser identifies the properties and reports the units of comparison calculated for each. The unit of comparison used on the form is price per square foot of gross living area, the price unit most commonly used by buyers and sellers of single-family residential properties in making their pricing decisions. The balance of the grid lists typical elements of comparison used in appraising single-family residential properties (e.g., date of sale, location) and provides space for recording market-extracted dollar adjustments for each, the net amount of the adjustments, and an adjusted sale price for each comparable.

In the final section of the analysis grid, the appraiser reports the details of any recorded sales of the subject or comparables within one year of the effective date of valuation.

| H72 | Address | The address of the subject and of each comparable property should include the name of the city, town, or community in which the property is located. It is helpful for the appraiser also to provide a numbered map reference above each address. These numbers will help readers of the report find the subject and the comparables on the location map provided as an attachment to the form. |

| H73 | Proximity to Subject | Distance should be expressed in blocks, fractions of a mile, and miles, e.g., "one-half block south of subject." Although there is no established standard on the acceptable distance between comparables and the subject, the appraiser should comment on any comparable properties located a substantial distance away from the subject. In urban and suburban areas, comparable properties are generally located in the same neighborhood or subdivision as the residence being appraised. The appraiser should consider how this entry relates to the neighborhood classification as urban, suburban, or rural, which was recorded in Section B27. |

| H74 | Sales Price | The total acquisition price of the subject property and each comparable should be recorded on this line. If a sale price is entered for the subject property, it should match the figure recorded on the front page of the form. To allow for valid comparison, the sale prices of the comparable properties should be within the same general value range as the subject. |

| H75 | Price/Gross Living Area | The price per square foot of gross living area is calculated by dividing the sale price of each comparable by the indicated square footage. If there is no sale price for the subject, this space should be left blank or a notation should be made to indicate that this calculation will be derived from the market. To facilitate comparison, the price per square foot of gross living area (GLA) of the comparable sales should be in the same general range as the unit value of the property being appraised. |

H76	**Data and/or Verification Sources**	In this space the appraiser reports the data and/or verification sources for the information used in the sales comparison analysis. One or more sources may be needed to confirm the sales data for each property adequately. The data source for the subject property could be listed as "personal investigation" or "property inspection" or the name of a verification source could be recorded. If a listing service is the data source for any of the comparables, the appraiser should include the listing number. If the data source is an agent, broker, or other participant in the transaction, that person's name and telephone number should be provided.

When the appraiser analyzes available data to select comparable sales, he or she begins to form certain conclusions about the general market, the subject property, and the likely relationship between the data and the property being appraised. Sales evidence cannot be analyzed in a vacuum. Rather, it is studied against a backdrop of information about the specific area and the specific type of residence. Basic sources of market data include the appraiser's files, Realtors®, other appraisers, managers, and lenders; multiple listing services and professional data services; public records on file with title companies; published news items; real estate publications; and government offices and assessor's records.

H77	**Sales or Financing Concessions**	The first value adjustment is concerned with any special sales or financing arrangements applied to the comparable properties. The "Sales or Financing Concessions" section in the subject column is shaded because this area is not to be completed. The appraiser records specific information on the financing of the subject property in Section A22 or in an addendum and Section H98 of the Sales Comparison Analysis. The appraiser does enter specific sales or financing information relating to the comparable sales, including the mortgage amount, interest rate, loan type, and any loan fees or concessions that the seller paid. If the space on the appraisal form is not sufficient, the adjustments can be made on the appraisal form and a detailed explanation presented in an addendum.

Some examples of sales or financing concessions are below-market financing, loan discount points, payment of closing costs or monthly mortgage payments, and inclusion of nonrealty items. The amount of negative adjustment to be made to a comparable sold with financing concessions is equal to the increase in the purchase price of the property attributable to the concessions. This amount is determined by the appraiser.

Adjustments must be made to the comparables for special or creative financing or sales concessions, but no adjustments are needed for costs that are normally paid by sellers as a result of tradition or law in the market area. These costs are easily identified because the seller pays them in virtually all transactions. Adjustments for special or creative financing can be made to a comparable property by comparing the financing to the financing terms offered by a third-party institutional lender not involved in the transaction. The adjustment should not be calculated mechanically, based on the dollar-for-dollar cost of the financing or concession. Instead, the adjustment should reflect the market's reaction to the financing or concessions and the appraiser's judgment.

The effect of sales concessions on sale prices can vary with the amount of the concessions and the characteristics of the market. The adjustments made should reflect the difference between the sale price of the comparable property and the price it would have sold for without the concessions. The dollar amount of the adjustment can then approximate the market's reaction to the concessions.

| H78 | **Date of Sale/Time** | On this line the appraiser enters the date of the sales contract and the settlement or closing date for each property. Only the month and year are provided unless the exact date is necessary for the reader of the report to understand a specific adjustment. If only the contract date is recorded, the appraiser must note whether the contract resulted in a settlement or closing. |

Time adjustments are important. They must be supported by market data and should be consistent with the appraiser's description of neighborhood value trends. The appraiser's objective is to measure and report any increase or decrease in value that occurred between the date the comparable property was transferred and the effective date of the appraisal.

Generally, comparables that are more than 12 months old are not acceptable. The appraiser may present them as additional sales data if desired. Several major lending institutions and agencies currently require that all comparable sales must have closed within six months of the effective date of valuation. The appraiser should provide sound reasons for using comparable sales that are more than six months old.

| H79 | **Location** | This adjustment reflects differences in perceived value arising from a property's location in a somewhat dissimilar, but competing, market area. A large location adjustment casts doubt on the validity and comparability of the sales selected. The appraiser should explain major adjustments and reconcile location adjustments with the information presented in the Location and Neighborhood Analysis sections of the report. The "Description" column should show entries of "good," "average," or "fair," based on comparisons with the subject and the information recorded on the front page of the form. |

The most valid and useful comparable sales are those located in the subject neighborhood near the property being appraised. Sales of houses in the immediate neighborhood usually require little or no adjustment for location.

| H80 | **Leasehold/Fee Simple** | The appraiser identifies the property rights held by title to the subject property and each comparable sale—i.e., leasehold or fee simple. The appraiser should, if possible, select comparable sales that involve the same property rights as the subject because in some areas a substantial difference in value may be ascribed to this feature alone. The appraiser |

should ensure that the property rights identified for the subject here are consistent with those reported in Section A14. A description of leasehold and fee simple property rights can be found in the discussion of that section.

| H81 | Site | An overall quality rating of "good," "average," "fair," or "poor" may be assigned to the subject property site and a comparison rating provided for the site of each comparable. The appraiser should consider site factors such as size, shape, topography, drainage, encroachments, easements, and any detrimental site conditions. |

The parcel size of the subject and each comparable can be entered in the left-hand portion of each column space followed by the quality rating. Parcel size may be described in square feet or as a fraction or percentage of an acre.

The site adjustments should reflect the size and physical characteristics of each comparable parcel as well as the relative utility or usable area of the subject and competing sites. Any unusual adjustments in this section should be adequately explained in Section H98.

| H82 | View | An overall rating of "good," "average," "fair," or "poor" is entered for the subject property and a comparison rating is recorded for each comparable sale. If appropriate, the appraiser may add descriptive terms such as "river," "mountain," or "wooded." The view amenity of a site may have a significant impact on property value and must be analyzed in relation to competing properties. If a large adjustment is needed for this feature, the appraiser must be able to justify and adequately explain it in the comments in Section H98. |

| H83 | Design and Appeal | In this space the appraiser considers the appeal of the exterior design, interior finishes, special features, and other characteristics that make a property more or less attractive to prospective buyers or otherwise affect its marketability. The appraiser analyzes the subject property as described on page one of the form and provides comparison ratings for each of the comparables—i.e., "good," "average," "fair," or "poor." Appropriate adjustments can then be made. |

| H84 | Quality of Construction | The appraiser considers the quality of materials and workmanship found in exterior walls, roof coverings, framing (walls, floors, and roof), finish, flooring, interior walls, trim, doors, hardware, plumbing and electrical systems, baths, kitchens, and mechanical equipment. The appraiser provides an overall quality rating for the subject property, commensurate with the description of the improvements presented in Section E, and assigns comparative ratings for each of the comparable properties. |

An adjustment for the quality of construction may sometimes be based on the actual cost to reproduce depreciated components. More often, however, this adjustment reflects the appraiser's perception of the market's acceptance of apparently superior or inferior construction. Major adjustments will call into question the basic comparability of the sale analyzed. Unusually large adjustments for quality should be well-documented and thoroughly explained.

| H85 | Age | The appraiser should report the actual, or chronological, age of the subject property and each comparable and make the necessary adjustments indicated by the market. If the subject or a comparable has been substantially modernized or upgraded, the effective age may be noted in parentheses to the right of the actual age. Any reference to effective age in this grid will require a comment describing the basis for the age assigned and the degree of modernization. |

| H86 | Condition | The appraiser judges the condition of the subject property to be "good," "average," "fair," or "poor." For the comparables, similar ratings or comparative ratings of "superior," "equal," or "inferior" are entered along with the adjustments indicated by the market. A reliable basis for a condition adjustment is the estimated cost to correct the deficiencies observed in the property. Any adjustment for condition that exceeds the reasonable cost to cure the deficiencies should be thoroughly explained. |

The appraiser should avoid duplication in developing this adjustment. Care must be taken to adjust only for factors that were not previously incorporated into the adjustment for age. Items of curable and incurable deterioration can be sensitive elements in this analysis.

| H87 | Above-Grade Room Count— Gross Living Area | The appraiser records the total number of finished, above-grade rooms, the number of bedrooms and baths, and the total, above-grade, square-foot living area (as calculated in the cost approach) for the subject and comparable sale properties. Adjustments for basement area are not treated here, but in Section H88. The room count entered in the subject column must correspond with the information calculated in the room list (E59) and the figures used in the building floor plan sketch. Differences in the room counts of the properties should be handled with separate adjustments which are displayed directly above the adjustment assigned to gross living area. Adjustments for room counts should be adequately supported with explanatory comments. |

The living area and room counts of the subject and the comparables should be similar. Adjusting the purchase price of a five-bedroom house for size and using it to estimate the value of a three-bedroom property is not a market-oriented comparison. Major differences between the property being appraised and the comparable property must be carefully analyzed and addressed.

| H88 | Basement and Finished Rooms Below Grade | The appraiser should report basement improvements such as finished recreation rooms in the subject and the comparables and calculate adjustments for any differences. If there is no basement or only a partial basement, this should be indicated. |

Sometimes basement rooms are finished without a building permit. The appraiser should indicate in the narrative comments whether an attempt was made to verify if permits were obtained for the finished rooms, or if visual inspection indicates that these rooms were or were not built in conformance to local building ordinances. Because basement rooms are usually not included as living area and are accorded separate value, adjustments for finished basements, guest quarters, "in-law" apartments, or other auxiliary living areas are usually based on their contribution to total property value rather than the calculated cost to construct.

| H89 | Functional Utility |

This entry relates to the efficiency of a building's design and factors such as layout, room size, and general livability. Any adjustment in this category must be carefully correlated with the Description of Improvements, Section E, and with any functional obsolescence allocated in the Cost Approach section. Comparison ratings of "good," "average," "fair," and "poor" or "superior," "equal," and "inferior" may be recorded for the comparable sale properties and appropriate adjustments made to reflect a typical buyer's reaction to these differences.

Trends in single-family home construction sometimes determine whether residences have features such as porches, balconies, fireplaces, separate dining rooms, large kitchens, entry halls, and family rooms. Standards for dwellings also vary with location and the income level of prospective tenants. To assess the functional utility of a residence, the appraiser should attempt to interpret the reactions of typical purchasers in the specific market area.

| H90 | Heating/Cooling |

Most residential heating systems used in the United States are a form of standard-quality, forced-air or gravity-air system. The adequacy of the system is a professional judgment based on property comparisons and interpretations of market behavior.

The presence or absence of air-conditioning and the type of unit found in the subject and comparable properties should be noted and adjustments should be made. Price adjustments should be based on market expectations of adequate heating and cooling systems for the locale and comparisons of the type and quality of units found in comparable properties. The entries recorded in the subject column should correspond to the information in Sections E61 and E62 on page one.

| H91 | Energy Efficient Items |

Fannie Mae underwriting guidelines suggest that lenders give special consideration to borrowers who are purchasing properties that are considered energy efficient or will be undergoing modifications to improve energy efficiency. This directive is predicated on the assumption that higher monthly housing expenses and debt payment ratios may be justified because the borrower will save on energy costs.

Any adjustment for energy-efficient items should be based on their specific contribution to the overall value of the property, e.g., the additional amount of money a typical purchaser would pay for the property because of its energy-efficient equipment or fixtures.

The information in the subject column should be correlated with Sections E58 and F67 on the front of the form.

| H92 | **Garage/Carport** | The appraiser should record and make adjustments for the garages or carports of the subject property and the comparables and their auto capacity. The increase or decrease in value attributable to this feature should be based on the contribution of the garage or carport to the overall value of the property, not on the cost of construction. |

If a garage has been converted into a family room or other type of living area, the appraiser must determine whether the improvement was completed in accordance with local building requirements. If a visual inspection reveals that permits were not issued, the customary procedure is to assign no value to the space as living area and allocate value assuming its use as a garage. The downward adjustment required may be based on the estimated cost to cure the deficiency, i.e., return the garage to its legal use, which normally entails reconverting the interior and reinstalling a garage door. If the garage has been converted in accordance with city permit procedure, the appraiser may grant it full value as a living area or assign it another value based on the compatibility of the interior with the rest of the house and the converted area's general conformance with the original detail and design of the residence.

If no garage or carport exits, the appraiser must comment on any resulting loss of value and confirm whether the property is in violation of any local ordinances requiring off-street and/or covered parking.

| H93 | **Porch, Patio, Deck, Fireplace(s), etc.** | The appraiser should record the presence or absence of porches, patios, decks, fireplaces, and other building or site improvements and made the necessary adjustments indicated by the market. Differences in maintenance and appearance should also be reflected. |

This category includes improvements that are usually valued as a lump sum based on their contribution to the overall value of the property. This contributory value reflects what the market will pay, i.e., how much the sale price is increased by inclusion of the specific items. Adjustments for these building components should be based on local market expectations and buyer preferences.

| H94 | **Fence, Pool, etc.** | Items such as driveways, fences, retaining walls, pools, and landscaping are usually considered site improvements. Sometimes cost data can serve as a guide to value, but these items frequently do not return |

their full cost upon resale. They are usually assigned a lump-sum value based on their contribution to the overall value of the property. The adjustments made should reflect the perceived market value of these site improvements based on local market expectations.

H95

This blank section is provided for the appraiser to include an additional element of comparison not specifically identified on the comparison grid. The appraiser may use it for comparison of a feature unique to the subject property or one of the comparable sales, if such a comparison is appropriate to the analysis.

H96   **Net Adjustment (Total)**

When all required adjustments have been calculated and recorded, the appraiser reports the net total plus or minus adjustment for all items. To be credible, the sales comparison approach must be based on a sufficient amount of verified comparable sales data and related market evidence. Selection of appropriate comparable properties minimizes both the need for and the size of required price adjustments. The sales comparison approach is credible because it involves direct measurement of current market conditions. When major adjustments are made to the sales data, however, market reaction is adjusted out and the appraiser's opinion is adjusted in.

As indicated previously, dollar adjustments should reflect the market's reaction to the differences in the properties, not necessarily the cost of the differences. Swimming pools, intercom systems, elaborately finished basements, and other special amenities generally do not add value commensurate with their cost to construct. Value is based on how much more a typical purchaser would pay for the property because it has a swimming pool, an intercom system, or a bowling alley in the basement.

Current Fannie Mae guidelines stipulate that, in general, the dollar amount of the net adjustment to each comparison property should not exceed 15% of the comparable property's sale price. The gross adjustment is calculated by adding together all of the individual adjustments regardless of whether they are negative or positive amounts. In certain circumstances, excessive adjustments may be warranted; the appraiser must, however, justify the analysis and explain why the particular comparable property was used. In all cases the appraiser must thoroughly research the market and identify, catalog, analyze, and report those sales that are most comparable to the residence being appraised.

H97   **Adjusted Sales Price of Comparable**

On this line the appraiser records the total adjusted sales price for each of the three comparable properties. The appraiser adds or subtracts the net total adjustment from the sales price of each comparable sale to arrive at a value indication for the subject property. The sales indicate an estimated value range for the subject property based on direct market comparison.

| H98 | **Comments on Sales Comparison** | This section is used to summarize and reconcile the adjusted values developed in the sales comparison grid. The indicators of value are analyzed for consistency and their relative strength in evaluating the typical purchaser's motivation in the market. Comments concerning which comparable sales provide the best indication of the value of the subject property provide support for the documentation and derivation of a single "most probable" value estimate. The appraiser must remember that this is not an averaging process and should indicate which comparable sale or set of comparable sales was given the most weight in the correlation analysis. The comments recorded here should provide a logical basis for the indicated value by the sales comparison approach.

In this section the appraiser can also provide additional information on details of the sales adjustments and other meaningful comments relating to the comparable sales analysis. |

| H99 | **Date, Price and Data Source for prior sales within year of appraisal** | The appraiser provides a one-year sales history of the subject property and each comparable sale used in the sales comparison analysis. Each history includes the date of sale, price, and verifying data source. |

| H100 | **Analysis of any current agreement of sale, option, or listing of subject property and analysis of any prior sales of subject and comparables within one year of the date of appraisal** | In this section the appraiser reports any market activity concerning the subject property or the comparable sales within the one-year period preceding the effective date of appraisal whether or not this activity resulted in a settlement. If no transfers or market activity occurred, many lenders are requesting that this fact be stated on these lines. |

| | **Standards Note** | Standards Rule 1-5 provides:

In developing a real estate appraisal, an appraiser must:

(a) consider and analyze any current Agreement of Sale, option, or listing of the property being appraised, if such information is available to the appraiser in the normal course of business;

(b) consider and analyze any prior sales of the property being appraised that occurred within the following time periods:

(i) one year for one- to four-family residential property; and

(ii) three years for all other property types;

(c) consider and reconcile the quality and quantity of data available and analyzed within the approaches used and the applicability or suitability of the approaches used. |

| H101 | **Indicated Value by Sales Comparison Approach** | The dollar amount of the reconciled value estimate should be recorded in the space provided. |

I102 Indicated Value by Income Approach (If Applicable)

Estimated Market Rent $_____ /Mo. x Gross Rent Multiplier_____ =$ _____

The income approach may be a valid measure of the market value of a residence if the subject property is located in a neighborhood where houses are commonly rented; it is generally not applicable in neighborhoods consisting primarily of owner-occupied houses. The typical home buyer does not base purchasing decisions on the income-generating potential of the property. Moreover, in owner-occupied areas, sufficient rental information is not available to support the income approach and provide a meaningful value indication.

Estimated Market Rent/Mo. The estimated monthly rent that the subject could be expected to generate if it were leased should be calculated and entered in this space. Because the market is the final judge of rental value, the appraiser should perform an economic rent survey to estimate an appropriate lease rate or determine if the existing rent of the subject property is consistent with the market. The tenant-occupied houses selected for analysis in the rental survey should be as closely comparable to the subject as possible. They should be located in the subject market area and rented at approximately the same time as the effective date of the appraisal. In most instances, the gross rent of the unfurnished residence is estimated on a monthly basis.

Gross Rent Multiplier. An appropriate monthly gross rent multiplier for the subject property is derived from the market and entered in this space. A gross rent multiplier is a factor that expresses the ratio between the sale price of a house and the gross rental income it produces as of the date of transfer. A gross rent multiplier is derived by dividing the sale price of a comparable property that was rented at the time of sale by its monthly rent.

A multiplier can be used as an indication of market value because it reflects a constant relationship between the gross monthly rent of a single-family residence and its sale price. The application of a rent multiplier in appraising houses is based on the presumption that value is related to the amount of rental income the property can be expected to generate.

To derive a multiplier, the appraiser should compare current sales of properties that are locationally and structurally similar to the subject. The rent produced by the comparable properties should be competitive in the market and consistent with the economic rent levels prevailing at the time of transfer. The appraiser should be certain to analyze enough sales to provide adequate support for a proper value conclusion.

Resulting Value. The estimated market rent of the subject property is multiplied by the gross rent multiplier to arrive at the indicated value by the income approach. This amount should be calculated and recorded in the space at the far right.

Figure 11. Indicated Value by Income Approach, Section I

INDICATED VALUE BY INCOME APPROACH (If Applicable) Estimated Market Rent $ _____ /Mo. x Gross Rent Multiplier _____ = $ _____ 1102

J	**Reconciliation**	In the Reconciliation section the appraiser's judgment is put to the test. The value indications developed from the three approaches to value must be weighed in light of their validity, accuracy, and applicability to the subject property.

Although the appraisal is to be reported on a standardized form, each property's characteristics and location are unique. In completing this section the appraiser has a final opportunity to discuss the subject property, the circumstances surrounding the valuation problem, and the application of the three approaches to value. |
| **J103** | **This appraisal is made "as is"; subject to repairs, alterations, inspections, or conditions...; subject to completion per plans and specifications.** | The appraiser should check the appropriate box to indicate whether the subject property was appraised "as is" or if the appraisal assumes completion of stipulated repairs, alterations, inspection, or other conditions to achieve the estimated value. Also, if the subject property is proposed or under construction, it should be noted that the valuation is subject to its satisfactory completion in accordance with the plans and specifications.

The term *inspection* as used in this section refers to property inspection by an outside party—i.e., someone other than the appraiser. When necessary, a professional opinion concerning building code requirements, nonconforming use, pest infestation, engineering considerations, or toxic or hazardous material problems should be included. |
| **J104** | **Conditions of Appraisal** | Here the appraiser itemizes the cost of necessary repairs, provides details on other conditions of the valuation, and comments on any previous section of the report. If the space provided is insufficient, an addendum should be attached.

This section is provided to conform with Standards Rule 2-1(c), which requires that all special appraisal provisions and conditions be identified in the report and their effect (if any) on the value of the property be reported. |
| **J105** | **Final Reconciliation** | This entry allows the appraiser to explain the relevance and validity of each valuation approach and to justify the final value estimate. The appraisal must be based on the definition of market value, certification, and limiting conditions that have been previously stated in the report.

The final step in the valuation process is to reconcile the indications of value into a single dollar figure. The nature of the reconciliation depends on the number of approaches used and the reliability of the value indications derived. The appraiser must consider the relative reliability and applicability of each approach when reconciling the value indications derived into a final estimate of defined value. A well-presented valuation analysis will allow the reader to understand the appraisal problem, interpret the data collected, and follow the reasoning that leads to the appraiser's conclusion of value. |

Figure 12. Reconciliation, Section J

This appraisal is made J103 ☐ "as is" ☐ subject to the repairs, alterations, inspections, or conditions listed below ☐ subject to completion per plans and specifications.

Conditions of Appraisal: J104 _____

Final Reconciliation: J105 _____
_____
_____

The purpose of this appraisal is to estimate the market value of the real property that is the subject of this report, based on the above conditions and the certification, contingent and limiting conditions, and market value definition that are stated in the attached Freddie Mac Form 439/Fannie Mae Form 1004B (Revised ___ J106 ___).

I (WE) ESTIMATE THE MARKET VALUE, AS DEFINED, OF THE REAL PROPERTY THAT IS THE SUBJECT OF THIS REPORT, AS OF (WHICH IS THE DATE OF INSPECTION AND THE EFFECTIVE DATE OF THIS REPORT) TO BE $ ___ J107 ___ .

APPRAISER: | **SUPERVISORY APPRAISER (ONLY IF REQUIRED):**

Signature _____ | Signature _____ | ☐ Did ☐ Did Not

Name _____ | Name _____ | Inspect Property

Date Report Signed _____ | Date Report Signed _____

State Certification # _____ State | State Certification # _____ State

Or State License # _____ State | Or State License # _____ State

68

The purpose of this appraisal is to estimate the market value of the real property that is the subject of this report, based on the above conditions and the certification, contingent and limiting conditions, and market value definition that are stated in the attached Freddie Mac Form 439/Fannie Mae Form 1004B (Revised _____).

This entry stipulates that the purpose of the appraisal is to estimate the market value of the real property. It is intended to require the appraiser to perform a separate analysis if personal property is being valued. It also ensures compliance with Standards Rule 2-2(c) ("state the purpose of the appraisal"), Standards Rule 2-2(d) ("define the value to be estimated") and Standards Rule 2-2(g) ("set forth all assumptions and limiting conditions that affect the analyses, opinions, and conclusions").

Fannie Mae Form 1004B should be attached as an addendum and the date printed at the bottom of that form should be entered in the space provided in this section for the date of revision.

Standards Note

In conformance with S.R. 2-2(e) of the Standards of Professional Appraisal Practice, a complete Statement of Limiting Conditions and Appraiser's Certification must be signed, dated, and attached to each report.

I (we) estimate the market value, as defined, of the real property that is the subject of this report, as of _____ (which is the date of inspection and the effective date of this report) to be $ _____ .

This entry indicates that the effective date of appraisal (the effective date of the report) is the date of property inspection. It is assumed that the appraisal is made as of a current date. On occasion the client may request that the effective date of appraisal be retrospective, specifying a time in the past such as the date of destruction or the time of death of one of the owners. In such a case the effective date is not the date of inspection and the wording on the form should be revised accordingly. If the effective date of appraisal is not the date of inspection, this should be explained and reported.

In this final section of the form, space is provided for the appraiser to record his or her state license or certification number and to acknowledge the roles of assistants in the valuation process and co-signers of the appraisal report. This statement (and the accompanying certification on the revised Form 1004B) allows an appraiser who has relied on the significant professional assistance of another in the performance of the appraisal or the preparation of the report to identify that individual and the specific tasks he or she performed in the Reconciliation section of the report and to certify that the named individual was qualified to perform the tasks completed.

Fannie Mae Compliance Note

Completion of this section will, in most states, provide sufficient compliance with the requirements and intent of the Real Estate Appraisal Reform Amendments (Title XI) of FIRREA for an appraisal report in which an unlicensed or uncertified appraiser, working as an employee or subcontractor of a licensed or certified appraiser, performs a significant amount of the appraisal work (or the entire appraisal if he or she is qualified to do so) as long as the appraisal report is signed by a licensed or certified "supervisory" appraiser. In such a case the supervisory appraiser must certify that he or she directly supervises the appraiser who prepared the appraisal report, has reviewed the appraisal report, agrees with the statements and conclusions of the appraiser, agrees to be bound by some of the same certifications that the appraiser made, and takes full responsibility for the appraisal report. The supervisory function just described would also apply to the appraisal reports of a state-licensed or state-certified appraiser that are co-signed by the employer or contractor if the lender or client requests that the supervisory relationship between the appraiser and employer or contractor be acknowledged (or if such an acknowledgment is traditional in the local area).

Standards Compliance Note

If an appraiser is performing a "review" function that is different from the relationship previously described, that individual must prepare a separate review report and attach it to the appraisal report being reviewed. This requirement would apply to a situation in which a lender chooses to delegate the appraisal management function to a specific appraiser or an appraisal service and one of the conditions of this delegation is that the appraiser or appraisal service will assume responsibility for the appraisal. This is consistent with the appraisal review function outlined in Standard 3 of the Uniform Standards of Professional Appraisal Practice and with the Residential Appraisal Review Report (Form 2000), which is the Fannie Mae appraisal review form.

Attachments to the URAR Form

The items listed here are general in nature and represent the minimum attachments normally required for most residential appraisals. The type and number of attachments needed are dictated by client requirements and the scope and character of the assignment. In some cases appropriate attachments will include standard forms such as a Satisfactory Completion Certificate or a Single-Family Comparable Rent Schedule.

Statement of Limiting Conditions and Appraiser's Certification (Freddie Mac Form 439/ Fannie Mae Form 1004B)

This standard certification page is required for all residential appraisal form reports. The document states the definition of market value used in the analysis, the certification of the professional ethics employed in performing the appraisal assignment, and the applicable contingent and limiting conditions. The attachment is to be signed by all the appraisers involved in performing the appraisal.

Exterior Perimeter Sketch

An exterior perimeter sketch of each floor of the living structure (or structures) and any other building improvements included in the valuation must be attached to the report. The sketch provides effective visual reinforcement for the description and measurements of the subject presented on the URAR form. Certain lenders also require that the sketch identify interior rooms or living units.

A scale drawing is not required. Many appraisers find that drawing the sketch on graph paper produces good results. Others prepare this attachment using one of the many computer graphics software programs now on the market.

Legal Description

As discussed in relation to Section A5 on page one of the form, the legal description may include a copy of a site map, public recording plat, tract map, or other legal document that unmistakably identifies the subject property.

Location Map

An area or neighborhood map can be included to establish the location of the subject within its immediate surroundings and in relation to the comparable sales used. Location maps are required by most clients. Rub-off transfers of arrows, numbers, and marker signs are commonly used for identifying properties on location maps because they are usually clearer than handwritten notations.

Photographic Attachments

The specific photographs required in an appraisal report vary with the needs of the client and the nature of the assignment. The following may be considered general minimum requirements.

The Subject Property

- For existing dwellings and those under construction, a minimum of three exterior photographs: one front view, one rear view, and one street scene as viewed from the subject
- One photograph of each site improvement addressed in the valuation section
- One photograph of each specific feature or condition—e.g., a site amenity or deficiency—to which the appraiser has given special attention in the report
- For a proposed dwelling, two or more photographs of the building site from different angles and a street scene as viewed from the construction point

Comparable Sales

- One front-view photograph of each comparable sale used in the sales comparison approach

Most professional appraisers use a 35-mm. camera and color film. Only clear, well-focused photographs are appropriate for inclusion in a report. Photographs should be mounted on separate sheets and clearly identified. All photographs of the subject property should be displayed first, followed by photos of the comparable sales in order of their presentation.

Freddie Mac Form 439/ Fannie Mae Form 1004B Appraisal Note

The expanded limiting conditions presented on the revised form include several clarifications:

- The existing use of the property will be used to allocate the value of the land and the improvements in the cost approach.
- An exterior sketch is attached to help the reader visualize the property and its site.
- The appraiser is not qualified in the field of environmental hazards.
- The appraisal is not an environmental assessment of the property.
- The appraiser is not responsible for any environmental conditions that do exist or for any engineering or testing that might be required.
- A value based on alterations, repairs, or satisfactory completion assumes that completion is accomplished in a workmanlike manner.
- The appraiser's written consent and approval must be obtained before the information in the appraisal, the appraiser's identity and firm, or the appraiser's designations can be communicated to the public.

Confidentiality is consistent with the Uniform Standards of Professional Appraisal Practice.

Changes in the appraiser's certification include the following:

- New certification that the report was performed in compliance with the Uniform Standards of Professional Appraisal Practice

- New certification stating that the appraiser was not required to report a predetermined value or direction in value that favors the client, is based on a requested minimum, is based on a specific value, or is needed to approve a mortgage
- New certification acknowledging that an estimate of reasonable time for exposure in the open market is a condition of the definition of market value and is consistent with the marketing time noted in the neighborhood section
- Expanded certification that the appraiser has no present or future interest in the property and his or her compensation is not dependent on the value
- Expanded certification that the appraiser prepared all conclusions or relied on *named* individuals for significant assistance
- Expanded certification confirming the appraiser's personal inspection of the interior and exterior of the subject and the exterior of the comparables, and acknowledging that the appraiser must report apparent or known adverse conditions
- Expanded certification requiring the supervisory appraiser who signs a report prepared by an employee or subcontractor to ensure compliance with the Uniform Standards of Professional Appraisal Practice

Statement of Limiting Conditions and Appraiser's Certification (Freddie Mac Form 439/ Fannie Mae Form 1004B)

DEFINITION OF MARKET VALUE: The most probable price which a property should bring in a competitive and open market under all conditions requisite to a fair sale, the buyer and seller, each acting prudently, knowledgeably and assuming the price is not affected by undue stimulus. Implicit in this definition is the consummation of a sale as of a specified date and the passing of title from seller to buyer under conditions whereby: (1) buyer and seller are typically motivated; (2) both parties are well informed or well advised, and each acting in what he considers his own best interest; (3) a reasonable time is allowed for exposure in the open market; (4) payment is made in terms of cash in U. S. dollars or in terms of financial arrangements comparable thereto; and (5) the price represents the normal consideration for the property sold unaffected by special or creative financing or sales concessions* granted by anyone associated with the sale.

*Adjustments to the comparables must be made for special or creative financing or sales concessions. No adjustments are necessary for those costs which are normally paid by sellers as a result of tradition or law in a market area; these costs are readily identifiable since the seller pays these costs in virtually all sales transactions. Special or creative financing adjustments can be made to the comparable property by comparisons to financing terms offered by a third party institutional lender that is not already involved in the property or transaction. Any adjustment should not be calculated on a mechanical dollar for dollar cost of the financing or concession but the dollar amount of any adjustment should approximate the market's reaction to the financing or concessions based on the appraiser's judgment.

STATEMENT OF LIMITING CONDITIONS AND APPRAISER'S CERTIFICATION

CONTINGENT AND LIMITING CONDITIONS: The appraiser's certification that appears in the appraisal report is subject to the following conditions:

1. The appraiser will not be responsible for matters of a legal nature that affect either the property being appraised or the title to it. The appraiser assumes that the title is good and marketable and, therefore, will not render any opinions about the title. The property is appraised on the basis of it being under responsible ownership.

2. The appraiser has provided a sketch in the appraisal report to show approximate dimensions of the improvements and the sketch is included only to assist the reader of the report in visualizing the property and understanding the appraiser's determination of its size.

3. The appraiser has examined the available flood maps that are provided by the Federal Emergency Management Agency (or other data sources) and has noted in the appraisal report whether the subject site is located in an identified Special Flood Hazard Area. Because the appraiser is not a surveyor, he or she makes no guarantees, express or implied, regarding this determination.

4. The appraiser will not give testimony or appear in court because he or she made an appraisal of the property in question, unless specific arrangements to do so have been made beforehand.

5. The appraiser has estimated the value of the land in the cost approach at its highest and best use and the improvements at their contributory value. These separate valuations of the land and improvements must not be used in conjunction with any other appraisal and are invalid if they are so used.

6. The appraiser has noted in the appraisal report any adverse conditions (such as, needed repairs, depreciation, the presence of hazardous wastes, toxic substances, etc.) observed during the inspection of the subject property or that he or she became aware of during the normal research involved in performing the appraisal. Unless otherwise stated in the appraisal report, the appraiser has no knowledge of any hidden or unapparent conditions of the property or adverse environmental conditions (including the presence of hazardous wastes, toxic substances, etc.) that would make the property more or less valuable, and has assumed that there are no such conditions and makes no guarantees or warranties, express or implied, regarding the condition of the property. The appraiser will not be responsible for any such conditions that do exist or for any engineering or testing that might be required to discover whether such conditions exist. Because the appraiser is not an expert in the field of environmental hazards, the appraisal report must not be considered as an environmental assessment of the property.

7. The appraiser obtained the information, estimates, and opinions that were expressed in the appraisal report from sources that he or she considers to be reliable and believes them to be true and correct. The appraiser does not assume responsibility for the accuracy of such items that were furnished by other parties.

8. The appraiser will not disclose the contents of the appraisal report except as provided for in the Uniform Standards of Professional Appraisal Practice.

9. The appraiser has based his or her appraisal report and valuation conclusion for an appraisal that is subject to satisfactory completion, repairs, or alterations on the assumption that completion of the improvements will be performed in a workmanlike manner.

10. The appraiser must provide his or her prior written consent before the lender/client specified in the appraisal report can distribute the appraisal report (including conclusions about the property value, the appraiser's identity and professional designations, and references to any professional appraisal organizations or the firm with which the appraiser is associated) to anyone other than the borrower; the mortgagee or its successors and assigns; the mortgage insurer; consultants; professional appraisal organizations; any state or federally approved financial institution; or any department, agency, or instrumentality of the United States or any state or the District of Columbia; except that the lender/client may distribute the property description section of the report only to data collection or reporting service(s) without having to obtain the appraiser's prior written consent. The appraiser's written consent and approval must also be obtained before the appraisal can be conveyed by anyone to the public through advertising, public relations, news, sales, or other media.

APPRAISER'S CERTIFICATION: The Appraiser certifies and agrees that:

1. I have researched the subject market area and have selected a minimum of three recent sales of properties most similar and proximate to the subject property for consideration in the sales comparison analysis and have made a dollar adjustment when appropriate to reflect the market reaction to those items of significant variation. If a significant item in a comparable property is superior to, or more favorable than, the subject property, I have made a negative adjustment to reduce the adjusted sales price of the comparable and, if a significant item in a comparable property is inferior to, or less favorable than the subject property, I have made a positive adjustment to increase the adjusted sales price of the comparable.

2. I have taken into consideration the factors that have an impact on value in my development of the estimate of market value in the appraisal report. I have not knowingly withheld any significant information from the appraisal report and I believe, to the best of my knowledge, that all statements and information in the appraisal report are true and correct.

3. I stated in the appraisal report only my own personal, unbiased, and professional analysis, opinions, and conclusions, which are subject only to the contingent and limiting conditions specified in this form.

4. I have no present or prospective interest in the property that is the subject of this report, and I have no present or prospective personal interest or bias with respect to the participants in the transaction. I did not base, either partially or completely, my analysis and/or the estimate of market value in the appraisal report on the race, color, religion, sex, handicap, familial status, or national origin of either the prospective owners or occupants of the subject property or of the present owners or occupants of the properties in the vicinity of the subject property.

5. I have no present or contemplated future interest in the subject property, and neither my current or future employment nor my compensation for performing this appraisal is contingent on the appraised value of the property.

6. I was not required to report a predetermined value or direction in value that favors the cause of the client or any related party, the amount of the value estimate, the attainment of a specific result, or the occurrence of a subsequent event in order to receive my compensation and/or employment for performing the appraisal. I did not base the appraisal report on a requested minimum valuation, a specific valuation, or the need to approve a specific mortgage loan.

7. I performed this appraisal in conformity with the Uniform Standards of Professional Appraisal Practice that were adopted and promulgated by the Appraisal Standards Board of The Appraisal Foundation and that were in place as of the efective date of this apraisal, with the exception of the departure provision of those Standards, which does not apply. I acknowledge that an estimate of a reasonable time for exposure in the open market is a condition in the definition of market value and the estimate I developed is consistent with the marketing time noted in the neighborhood section of this report, unless I have otherwise stated in the reconciliation section.

8. I have personally inspected the interior and exterior areas of the subject property and the exterior of all properties listed as comparables in the appraisal report. I further certify that I have noted any apparent or known adverse conditions in the subject improvements, on the subject site, or on any site within the immediate vicinity of the subject property of which I am aware and have made adjustments for these adverse conditions in my analysis of the property value to the extent that I had market evidence to support them. I have also commented about the effect of the adverse conditions on the marketability of the subject property.

9. I personally prepared all conclusions and opinions about the real estate that were set forth in the appraisal report. If I relied on significant professional assistance from any individual or individuals in the performance of the appraisal or the preparation of the appraisal report, I have named such individual(s) and disclosed the specific tasks performed by them in the reconciliation section of this appraisal report. I certify that any individual so named is qualified to perform the tasks. I have not authorized anyone to make a change to any item in the report; therefore, if an unauthorized change is made to the appraisal report, I will take no responsibility for it.

SUPERVISORY APPRAISER'S CERTIFICATION: If a supervisory appraiser signed the appraisal report, he or she certifies and agrees that: I directly supervise the appraiser who prepared the appraisal report, have reviewed the appraisal report, agree with the statements and conclusions of the appraiser, agree to be bound by the appraiser's certifications numbered 4 through 7 above, and am taking full responsibility for the appraisal and the appraisal report.

ADDRESS OF PROPERTY APPRAISED: _____

APPRAISER: SUPERVISORY APPRAISER: (only if required):

Signature: _____   Signature: _____
Name: _____   Name: _____
Date Signed: _____   Date Signed: _____
State Certification #: _____   State Certification #: _____
or State License #: _____   or State License #: _____
State: _____   State: _____
Expiration Date of Certification or License: Expiration Date of Certification or License:

☐ Did ☐ Did Not Inspect Property

Conclusions

The Uniform Residential Appraisal Report form is increasingly accepted and employed by users of residential appraisals. Unfortunately, standardized forms have inherent shortcomings. A report form provides a method for communicating, not conducting, an appraisal analysis. The use of standard forms does not mean that the quality of appraisal reports has become standardized.

Appraisers who prepare form reports should remember that the form can only reflect a valid appraisal analysis if it is properly completed and documented and all necessary supplemental material is attached. No form can replace the professional judgment and experience of the individual appraiser, which are essential to a proper value estimate.

Appendix

1. Fannie Mae Announcement
2. Freddie Mac Form 72/Fannie Mae Form 1025
3. Freddie Mac Form 465/Fannie Mae Form 1073
4. Employee Relocation Council Residential Appraisal Report Form
5. Guide Notes to the Standards of Professional Appraisal Practice
   - Guide Note 2. Cash Equivalency in Value Estimates in Accordance with Standards Rule 1-2(b)
   - Guide Note 3. The Use of Form Appraisal Reports for Residential Property
   - Guide Note 8. Consideration of Hazardous Substances in the Appraisal Process
6. Statements on Appraisal Standards adopted by the Appraisal Standards Board
   - Statement No. 3. Retrospective Value Estimates
   - Statement No. 4. Prospective Value Estimates
   - Statement No. 5. Confidentiality Rule of the Ethics Provision
   - Statement No. 6. Reasonable Exposure Time in Market Value Estimates
7. Advisory Opinions adopted by the Appraisal Standards Board
   - Advisory Opinion G-1. Sales History
   - Advisory Opinion G-2. Inspection of Subject Property Real Estate
   - Advisory Opinion G-4. Standards Rule 1-5(b)
   - Advisory Opinion G-7. Marketing Time Estimates
8. Standards Rules 2-1, 2-2, 2-3, and 2-5

Announcement

• Selling
  Servicing

This announcement amends the guide(s) indicated. Please keep it for reference until we issue a formal change.

Subject   Revised Appraisal Report Forms

Last December, we released revised single-family appraisal report forms and asked appraisers and lenders to use them for a four-month test period. The revisions to the forms resulted from a joint review effort that included Fannie Mae, Freddie Mac, the Department of Housing and Urban Development, the Department of Veterans Affairs, and an appraisal industry working group (which consisted of representatives from The Appraisal Foundation Advisory Council; Appraisal Standards Advisory Council; Mortgage Bankers Association of America; Mortgage Insurance Companies of America; American Bankers Association; Savings and Community Bankers of America; Farmers Home Administration; the staff of the Appraisal Subcommittee of the Federal Financial Institutions Examination Council; and representatives of several appraisal data collection, form, and software companies). Representatives of the Appraisal Standards Board of The Appraisal Foundation also reviewed the revised forms to assure that they were in compliance with the Uniform Standards of Professional Appraisal Practice. The overall consensus of those who reviewed and used the revised forms during the test period was that they represented an improvement over the existing forms. We would like to thank not only the members of the working group, but also the many appraisers and lenders that took the time and effort to review or use the test forms and to provide comments and recommendations to us.

Based on the comments we received, we made several revisions that resulted in improvements to the test forms. The resulting revised <u>Uniform Residential Appraisal Report</u> (Form 1004) and <u>Statement of Limiting Conditions and Appraiser's Certification</u> (Form 1004B) must be used for appraisals of single-family properties made on and after January 1, 1994. Until then, either the current or test version of the forms may be used. However, lenders and appraisers that choose to use the revised forms immediately may do so.

<u>Explanation of Revisions</u>

Specific revisions to the <u>Uniform Residential Appraisal Report</u> (Form 1004) and the <u>Statement of Limiting Conditions and Appraiser's Certification</u> (Form 1004B) were designed to address issues

Announcement

related to the Uniform Standards of Professional Appraisal Practice, the appraiser's responsibility for noting apparent or known adverse conditions in the appraisal report, the role of a supervisory or review appraiser, and deficiencies in the current forms that have been identified by appraisers, lenders, and investors.

The changes that are reflected in the revised Forms 1004 and 1004B recognize the Uniform Standards of Professional Appraisal Practice that were adopted and promulgated by the Appraisal Standards Board of The Appraisal Foundation (with the exception of the departure provision of those standards, which does not apply) as the minimum appraisal standards for the appraisal industry. Fannie Mae will continue to have its own separate appraisal requirements to supplement the minimum requirements of the Uniform Standards of Professional Appraisal Practice because we believe that is necessary to assure that all of our specific concerns are addressed for any given appraisal. The revised Form 1004 is designed in a way that results in an appraiser being able to be in full compliance with our requirements if he or she addresses all of the specific information on the form and presents the applicable data accurately and completely. We require appraisers to prepare the appraisal report in a manner that clearly reflects the results of their investigation and analysis and to provide the rationale for their estimate of market value, going beyond any limitations of the form by providing additional comments and exhibits when they are needed to support their conclusions.

We currently allow the <u>Certification and Statement of Limiting Conditions</u> (Form 1004B) either to be on file with the lender or to be submitted as an exhibit to each individual appraisal report form. Because we are modifying our appraisal standards to specifically acknowledge the Uniform Standards of Professional Appraisal Practice as the minimum standards of the appraisal industry, we will require the revised <u>Statement of Limiting Conditions and Appraiser's Certification</u> (Form 1004B) to be signed and submitted by the appraiser as an exhibit to the appraisal report form for each appraisal assignment. We believe that any issues related to the reasons appraisers felt it was necessary to make additions or deletions to the certification and statement of limiting conditions on Form 1004B in the past have been addressed in the revised form; therefore, we will no longer permit any changes to be made to the form. However, we will permit the appraiser to make additional certifications (but not limiting conditions) on a separate form or page. Among other things, acceptable additional certifications might include those required by state law or those related to the appraiser's continuing education or membership in an appraisal organization(s). We will continue

Announcement

to hold lenders accountable for reviewing any additional certifications made by an appraiser since we will not purchase a mortgage if the appraiser's additional certifications conflict with the standard certifications on Form 1004B or with any of our policies.

Beginning January 1, 1994, the revised Statement of Limiting Conditions and Appraiser's Certification (Form 1004B) must be used in connection with appraisals prepared for condominium units and two- to four-family properties. To acknowledge that the current version of the Form 1004B was used, an appraiser must modify the Appraisal Report - Individual Condominium or PUD Unit (Form 1073) by striking the earlier revision date for Form 1004B that appears on the form and replacing it with the current revision date (June, 1993) and modify the Small Residential Income Property Appraisal Report (Form 1025) by entering the current revision date (June, 1993) in the space provided on that form.

Attachments 1 and 2 provide explanations of the major changes and modifications made to the appraisal report forms and discuss any significant issues that were raised during the development and testing of the forms. Attachment 1 addresses the modifications to the Uniform Residential Appraisal Report (Form 1004); Attachment 2 addresses the modifications to the Statement of Limiting Conditions and Appraiser's Certification (Form 1004B). Camera-ready copy of both forms is attached at the end of this Announcement.

Computer-Generated Versions of Form 1004

Appraisers and lenders may use the attached camera-ready copy of the Uniform Residential Appraisal Report (Form 1004) to produce a supply of forms or they may reproduce forms individually as they are needed by using computer software programs designed for that purpose. Although we made every effort to expand the space for comments, many appraisers and lenders that participated in the review of the forms felt that the space provided still might not be adequate for comments since the amount and location of any required additional space varies on a case-by-case basis. To accommodate this concern, we will accept a Form 1004 that is generated by software programs with expandability features that allow increases in any of areas of the form that call for the insertion of narrative comments areas when the appraiser believes that this is necessary to accommodate a particular appraisal assignment. (The expansion must not, however, result in the "Sales Comparison Analysis" section being separated so that it appears on two pages.)

Regardless of whether the appraiser uses a two-page format or a computer-generated expandable format, we require that the sequence of the information on the Form 1004, as well as all of the specific

Announcement

Uniform Residential Appraisal Report (Form 1004)

The appraisal report form is designed to provide a concise format for presenting both the appraiser's description and analysis of the subject property and the valuation analysis leading to the estimate of market value. The modifications to the Uniform Residential Appraisal Report (Form 1004) are designed to enable the appraiser to present these analyses in a cogent and informative manner, using the additional space provided to insert clarifying comments or points of emphasis.

The revised form consists of ten basic sections -- subject, neighborhood, PUD, site, description of improvements, comments, cost approach, sales comparison analysis, income approach and reconciliation. Some of the more important changes to these sections are discussed below.

Subject Section   The "subject" section was modified to:

- include new entries for assessor's parcel number, special assessments, borrower's name, appraiser's name and address, as well as a new "occupant" entry that has convenient boxes that the appraiser checks to indicate whether the property was owner-occupied, tenant-occupied, or vacant as of the date of his or her inspection;

- separate the "property rights appraised" entry into two parts, one in which the appraiser indicates whether the property rights appraised are "fee simple" or "leasehold" and one in which the appraiser addresses whether the subject property is located in a PUD or condominium project. [Note: This form is generally used for appraisals on condominium units only for FHA-insured or VA-guaranteed mortgages. However, we will accept appraisals of detached condominium units on Form 1004 if the condominium project does not contain any common area improvements (other than greenbelts, private streets, and parking areas) and the appraiser includes an adequate description of the project and information about the owners' association fees and the quality of the project maintenance.]; and

- delete the obsolete reference to de minimis PUD (Note: We eliminated the concept of de minimis PUD when we redefined planned unit developments in 1989.) If the appraiser indicates that the subject property is located in a PUD, we require information about the unit's owners' association fees in this section and specific information about the project in the new PUD section.

Announcement

Neighborhood Section

The "neighborhood" section was modified to reinforce the appraiser's purpose for performing a neighborhood analysis, which is to identify the area — based on common characteristics or trends — that is subject to the same influences as the subject property. The sales prices of comparable properties in the identified area should reflect the positive and negative influences of the neighborhood. The results of the neighborhood analysis will enable the appraiser to define the area from which to select comparables, to understand market preferences and price patterns, to reach conclusions about the highest and best use of the subject property site, to examine the effect of different locations within the neighborhood, to determine the influence of nearby land uses, and to identify any other value influences affecting the neighborhood.

The modifications to the neighborhood section include the creation of new entries to describe

- neighborhood boundaries and characteristics;

- factors that affect the marketability of the properties in the neighborhood; and

- market conditions in the subject neighborhood (including support for the conclusions related to the trend of property values, demand/supply and marketing time).

One of the more important modifications to this section was the elimination of the neighborhood analysis rating grid. This change should result in the appraiser focusing on describing the various components of a neighborhood and reporting the factors that have an impact on value in the space provided for narrative comments in the report, rather than trying to develop a "relative" rating for the neighborhood.

PUD Section

A Planned Unit Development (PUD) is a project (or subdivision) that includes common property and improvements that are owned and maintained by an owners' association for the use and benefit of the individual units in the project (or subdivision). We classify a project (or subdivision) as a PUD if each unit owner's membership in the owners' association is automatic and nonseverable and the owners' association has the right to impose mandatory assessments. (We do not consider zoning to be a basis for classifying a project or subdivision as a PUD.)

This new "PUD" section was created to enable the appraiser to address the basic information about the project when the property being appraised is in a planned unit development. Information that

Announcement

the appraiser is asked to provide includes a description of the project (including a description of the common elements and recreational facilities and an indication of whether the developer/builder is in control of the owner's association) and the approximate total number of units in the project and the approximate total number of units for sale in the project. The creation of this new section should generally eliminate the need for attaching an addendum to the form for appraisals of units in established PUD projects. However, it may still be necessary to use an addendum for appraisals related to attached units in a new PUD project for which the developer is still in control of the owners' association, in order to satisfy the specific eligibility requirements we have for this type of project (see Part VIII, Sections 402 and 403, of the Selling Guide).

Site Section

Modifications to the "site" section include both clarifications to existing entries and the addition of new entries. New entries were created for the appraiser to

- indicate the subject property's compliance with zoning, by checking one of the convenient boxes (legal use; legal, but nonconforming use; illegal use; or no zoning), and

- address whether the subject community is in a FEMA Special Flood Hazard Area and to indicate the FEMA zone, map date, and map number for all appraisals of properties in such areas.

The clarifications to existing entries included specifying that the "FEMA Flood Hazard" entry relates only to 100-year flood plain areas and explaining that the appraiser's determination about the "highest and best use" of the property should reflect the property's use "as improved."

Description of Improvements Section

The "description of improvements" section represents a significant streamlining of the information necessary to describe the improvements. One of the major changes was the elimination of the improvement analysis rating in order to emphasize that the appraiser should adequately address the condition of the improvements, needed repairs, quality of construction, etc. by providing meaningful comments, instead of marking "relative" ratings. Other modifications included the elimination of the requirement to report the estimated remaining economic and physical life, the addition of new entries for amenities, and a significantly improved format for reporting car storage.

Announcement

Comments Section

The "comments" portion of this section includes a new entry in which the appraiser must address adverse environmental conditions (such as, but not limited to, hazardous wastes, toxic substances, etc.) that are present in the improvements, on the site, or in the immediate vicinity of the subject property. This addition clarifies the appraiser's responsibility to report what he or she became aware of through the inspection of the property and the normal research involved in performing the appraisal. (Note: See Attachment 2 for related significant modifications that were made to the certification and statement of limiting conditions regarding the appraiser's inspection and the acknowledgement of adverse conditions.)

Cost Approach Section

The "cost approach" section was modified to include a new area for comments on the cost approach (by eliminating the space dedicated to the building sketch on the current version of the form). The entry for the appraiser's estimate of the site value is now located above the estimated reproduction cost-new of improvements. Appraisers may continue to show the square foot (size) calculation for the property in this area or they may indicate it on the exterior building sketch of the improvements that we require as an exhibit to each appraisal report.

Sales Comparison Analysis Section

The "sales comparison analysis" adjustment grid was modified to include an entry in which the appraiser reports the data and/or verification sources for the comparable sales (to assure compliance with the Uniform Standards requirement that the appraiser verify comparable market data). An appraiser may use a single source for his or her data and verifications or may use multiple sources if they are needed to adequately verify the comparable sales. The quality of the data available for single-family residential properties varies from source to source and from one locality to another. In view of this, a single data source may be adequate if the appraiser uses a source that provides quality sales data that is confirmed or verified by closed or settled transactions. On the other hand, if the appraiser's basic data source does not confirm or verify the sales data, the appraiser will need to use additional sources.

We added space after the adjustment grid to report the date, price, and data source for prior sales of the subject property and comparable sales within one year of the effective date of the appraisal. (Note: The data source for the prior sales of the subject and the comparables does not have to be the same as the appraiser's data and/or verification source that was reported at the top of the adjustment grid.)

A new area for narrative comments was created for the appraiser's analysis of any prior sales of the subject property and the comparables, as well as of any current agreement of sale, option, or listing

Announcement

of the subject property (to assure compliance with the Uniform Standards). The space used for providing narrative comments related to the sales comparison analysis was also significantly expanded.

Reconciliation Section

Several significant modifications were made to the "reconciliation" section. We clarified that the purpose of the appraisal is to estimate the market value of the <u>real</u> property that is the subject of the report, which means that the appraiser would need to perform a separate analysis if he or she was appraising personal property. We made two modifications that are designed to assure the appraiser's compliance with the Uniform Standards -- one related to requiring the appraiser's certification and statement of limiting conditions and the definition of market value to be attached to each appraisal report (instead of allowing the appraiser to file the certification with the client) and one related to requiring the appraiser to report both the date of the appraisal report (which is the date the report is signed) and the effective date of the report (which is the date of the appraiser's inspection of the subject property), as opposed to requiring only the effective date of the report as we currently do.

We also included a space for the appraiser to note his or her state license or certification number and to acknowledge the roles of assistants in the appraisal process and co-signers of the appraisal report. This change (and the accompanying certification in the revised Form 1004B) allows an appraiser who has relied on significant professional assistance from any individual(s) in the performance of the appraisal or the preparation of the report to name the individual(s) and the specific tasks performed in the "Reconciliation" section of the report and to certify that the named individual(s) are qualified to perform the tasks. These modifications also acknowledge that, in some states, the appraisal report will still be viewed as complying with the intent of the Real Estate Appraisal Reform Amendments (Title XI) of FIRREA if an unlicensed or uncertified appraiser who is working as an employee or subcontractor of a licensed or certified appraiser performs a significant amount of the appraisal (or the entire appraisal if he or she is qualified to do so) -- as long as the appraisal report is signed by a licensed or certified "supervisory" appraiser. (The supervisory appraiser must certify that he or she directly supervises the appraiser who prepared the appraisal report, has reviewed the appraisal report, agrees with the statements and conclusions of the appraiser, agrees to be bound by some of the same certifications that the appraiser made, and takes full responsibility for the appraisal report.) The supervisory function just described would also apply when the appraisal reports of a state-licensed or -certified appraiser are co-signed by his or her employer or

Announcement

contractor if the lender or client requests that the supervisory relationship between the appraiser and his or her employer or contractor be acknowledged (or if such an acknowledgment is traditional in the locality).

If an appraiser is performing a "review" function that is different from the relationship(s) described above, he or she must prepare a separate review report and attach it to the appraisal report being reviewed. For instance, this approach would apply when a lender chooses to delegate the appraisal management function to a specific appraiser or an appraisal service and one of the conditions of this delegation is that the specific appraiser or appraisal service will assume responsibility for the appraisal. This approach is consistent with the appraisal review function outlined in Standard 3 of the Uniform Standards of Professional Appraisal Practice and with the <u>Residential Appraisal Review Report</u> (Form 2000), which is our appraisal review form.

Announcement

Statement of Limiting Conditions and Appraiser's Certification (Form 1004B)

The Uniform Standards of Professional Appraisal Practice specifically requires the appraiser's certification to be included in each individual appraisal report. Form 1004B was revised to reflect this and to improve clarity. Key changes include:

- an expanded contingent and limiting condition clarifying that the appraiser is not an expert in the field of environmental hazards and the appraisal report is not to be considered an environmental assessment of the property, and acknowledging that the appraiser is responsible for noting any adverse conditions (such as hazardous wastes, toxic substances, etc.) observed during the inspection of the subject property or that he or she became aware of during the normal research involved in performing the appraisal;

- a new certification stating that the appraiser has examined flood maps provided by the Federal Emergency Management Agency (or other data sources) and has noted whether the subject property is located in a Special Flood Hazard Area. We also clarified that the appraiser makes no guarantees regarding this determination since he or she is not a surveyor;

- an expanded certification clarifying the parties to whom the lender/client specified in the appraisal report can distribute the appraisal report;

- a new certification addressing the appraiser's research and selection of comparable sales and adjustments in the sales comparison approach to value;

- an expanded certification stating that the appraiser has no present or contemplated future interest in the property (or the participants in the transaction) and that neither his or her current or future employment nor compensation for performing the appraisal is contingent on the appraised value of the property;

- an expanded certification stating that the appraiser did not base, either partially or completely, his or her analysis and/or estimate of market value in the appraisal report on the race, color, religion, sex, handicap, familial status, or national origin of either the prospective owners or occupants of the subject property or of the present owners or occupants of the properties in the immediate vicinity of the subject property;

Announcement

- a new certification stating that the appraiser was not required to report a predetermined value or direction in value that favors the cause of the client or any related party, the amount of the value estimate, the attainment of a specific result, or the occurrence of a subsequent event in order to receive his or her compensation for performing the appraisal.(The appraiser must also certify that he or she did not base the appraisal report on a requested minimum valuation, a specific valuation, or the need to approve a specific mortgage loan.);

- a new certification stating that the appraisal report was performed in compliance with the Uniform Standards of Professional Appraisal Practice (with the exception of the departure provision which does not apply);

- a new certification acknowledging that an estimate of reasonable time for exposure in the open market is a condition of the definition of market value and clarifying that the appraiser's estimate of reasonable exposure time is consistent with the marketing time noted in the "Neighborhood" section (unless otherwise noted in the "Reconciliation" section of the report);

- an expanded certification addressing the appraiser's personal inspection of the interior and exterior of the subject property, the exterior of all properties listed as comparables in the appraisal report, and his or her responsibility to note apparent or known adverse conditions that he or she is aware of in the subject improvements, on the subject site, or on any site within the immediate vicinity of the subject property;

- an expanded certification stating that the appraiser either prepared all conclusions and opinions about the real estate that were set forth in the appraisal report or relied on significant professional assistance from another person in the performance of the appraisal or the preparation of the report. (In the latter instance, the appraiser must name in the appraisal report individuals providing the assistance, disclose the specific tasks performed by such individuals, and certify that the individuals are qualified to perform the tasks they did); and

- a new certification clarifying the role of the "supervisory appraiser" (which we currently refer to as a "review appraiser") who signs an appraisal report prepared by an employee or subcontractor that he or she directly supervises, to assure compliance with the guidance from the Appraisal Standards Board of The Appraisal Foundation and the Appraisal Reform Amendments (Title XI) of FIRREA.

Freddie Mac Form 72\Fannie Mae Form 1025

Property Description & Analysis

SMALL RESIDENTIAL INCOME PROPERTY APPRAISAL REPORT   File No. _____

Subject

Property address _____	**Lender discretionary use**
City _____ County _____ State _____ Zip code _____	Sale price $ _____
Legal description _____	Gross monthly rent $ _____
Owner / occupant _____ Tax year _____ R.E. taxes $ _____	Closing date _____
Sale price $ _____ Date of sale _____ Census tract _____ Map reference _____	Mortgage amount $ _____
Property rights appraised ☐ Fee simple ☐ Leasehold ☐ Condominium or ☐ PUD HOA $ ____ / Mo	Mortgage type _____
Borrower _____ Project Name _____	Discount points and other concessions _____
Loan charges / concessions to be paid by seller $ _____	Paid by seller $ _____
Lender / client _____	Source _____
Appraiser _____	

Neighborhood

Location	☐ Urban	☐ Suburban	☐ Rural
Built up	☐ Over 75%	☐ 25-75%	☐ Under 25%
Growth rate	☐ Rapid	☐ Stable	☐ Slow
Property values	☐ Increasing	☐ Stable	☐ Declining
Demand / supply	☐ Shortage	☐ In balance	☐ Over supply
Marketing time	☐ Under 3 mos.	☐ 3-6 mos.	☐ Over 6 mos.

Predominant occupancy
☐ Owner
☐ Tenant
☐ Vacant (0-5%)
☐ Vacant (over 5%)

Single family housing
PRICE $(000)   AGE (yrs)
Low _____
High _____
Predominant _____

Neighborhood analysis	Good	Avg.	Fair	Poor
Employment stability	☐	☐	☐	☐
Convenience to employment	☐	☐	☐	☐
Convenience to shopping	☐	☐	☐	☐
Convenience to schools	☐	☐	☐	☐
Adequacy of public transportation	☐	☐	☐	☐
Recreation facilities	☐	☐	☐	☐
Adequacy of utilities	☐	☐	☐	☐
Property compatibility	☐	☐	☐	☐
Protection from detrimental cond.	☐	☐	☐	☐
Police & fire protection	☐	☐	☐	☐
General appearance of properties	☐	☐	☐	☐
Appeal to market	☐	☐	☐	☐

Typical 2-4 family bldg. Type _____
No. stories _____ No. units _____
Age _____ yrs. Condition _____
Typical rents $ _____ to $ _____
☐ Increasing ☐ Stable ☐ Declining
Est. neighborhood apt. vacancy _____ %
☐ Increasing ☐ Stable ☐ Declining

Present land use %
One family _____
2-4 family _____
Multifamily _____
Commercial _____
Industrial _____
Vacant _____

Land use change
☐ Not likely
☐ Likely
☐ In process
To : _____

2-4 family housing
PRICE $(000)   AGE (yrs)
Low _____
High _____
Predominant _____

Rent controls ☐ Yes * ☐ No ☐ Likely *

Note : Race and the racial composition of the neighborhood are not considered reliable appraisal factors.

Description of neighborhood boundaries : _____

Description of those factors, favorable or unfavorable, that affect marketability (including neighborhood stability, appeal, property conditions, vacancies, * rent control, etc.).
_____

The following available listings represent the most current, similar, and proximate competitive properties to the subject property in the subject neighborhood. This analysis is intended evaluate the inventory currently on the market competing with the subject property in the subject neighborhood and recent price and marketing time trends affecting the subject prope (Listings outside the subject neighborhood are not considered applicable). The listing comparables can be the rental or sale comparables if they are currently for sale.

ITEM	SUBJECT	COMPARABLE LISTING NO. 1	COMPARABLE LISTING NO. 2	COMPARABLE LISTING NO. 3
Address				
Proximity to subject				
Listing price	$	☐ Unf. ☐ Furn.$	☐ Unf. ☐ Furn.$	☐ Unf. ☐ Furn.$
Approximate GBA				
Data source				
# Units/Tot.rms/BR/BA				
Approximate year built				
Approx. days on market				

Comparison of listings to subject property : _____

Reconciliation : Description and analysis of the general market conditions that affect 2-4 family properties in the subject neighborhood (including the above neighborhood indicators of rate, property values, demand / supply, and marketing time) and the prevalence and impact in the subject / market area regarding loan discounts, interest buydowns, and conces identification of trends in listing prices, average days on market and any change over past year, etc. : _____

Site

Dimensions _____	Topography _____
Site area _____ Corner lot ☐ No ☐ Yes	Size _____
Specific zoning classification and description _____	Shape _____
Zoning compliance : ☐ Legal ☐ Legal nonconforming (Grandfathered use) ☐ Illegal ☐ No zoning	Drainage _____
Highest & best use as improved : ☐ Present use ☐ Other use (explain) _____	View _____
	Landscaping _____

Utilities	Public	Other	Off-site Improvements	Type	Public	Private
Electricity	☐		Street		☐	☐
Gas	☐		Curb / gutter		☐	☐
Water	☐		Sidewalk		☐	☐
Sanitary sewer	☐		Street lights		☐	☐
Storm sewer	☐		Alley		☐	☐

Driveway _____
Apparent easements _____
FEMA Special flood hazard area ☐ Yes * ☐ No
* FEMA Zone/Map Date _____
* FEMA Map No. _____

Comments (apparent adverse easements, encroachments, special assessments, slide areas, illegal or legal nonconforming zoning, use, etc.) : _____

Freddie Mac Form 72\Fannie Mae Form 1025
—continued

Property Description & Analysis, continued   **SMALL RESIDENTIAL INCOME PROPERTY APPRAISAL REPORT**   File No.

Description of improvements

General description
- Units / bldgs. _____ /
- Stories _____
- Type (det. / att.) _____
- Design (style) _____
- Existing / proposed _____
- Under construction _____
- Year Built _____
- Effective age (yrs.) _____

Exterior description (Materials / condition)
- Foundation _____
- Exterior walls _____
- Roof surface _____
- Gutters & dwnspts. _____
- Window type _____
- Storm sash/Screens _____
- Manufactured housing * ☐ Yes ☐ No
- *(Complies with the HUD Manufactured Housing Construction and Safety Standards.)

Foundation
- Slab _____
- Crawl space _____
- Sump Pump _____
- Dampness _____
- Settlement _____
- Infestation _____
- Basement _____ % of 1st floor area
- Basement finish _____

Insulation (R-value if known)
- ☐ Roof _____
- ☐ Ceiling _____
- ☐ Walls _____
- ☐ Floor _____
- ☐ None _____
- Adequacy _____
- Energy efficient items : _____

Units	Level(s)	Foyer	Living	Dining	Kitchen	Den	Family rm.	#Bedrooms	#Baths	Laundry	Other	Sq.ft/unit	Total ☐ /

Improvements contain : _____ Rooms ; _____ Bedroom(s) ; _____ Bath(s) ; _____ Square feet of GROSS BUILDING AREA

GROSS BUILDING AREA (GBA) IS DEFINED AS THE TOTAL FINISHED AREA (INCLUDING COMMON AREAS) OF THE IMPROVEMENTS BASED UPON EXTERIOR MEASUREMENTS.

Surfaces (Materials / condition)
- Floors _____
- Walls _____
- Trim / finish _____
- Bath floor _____
- Bath wainscot _____
- Doors _____
- Fireplace(s) # _____

Heating
- Type _____
- Fuel _____
- Condition _____
- Adequacy _____

Cooling
- Central _____
- Other _____
- Condition _____
- Adequacy _____

Kitchen equip. (# / unit-Cond.)
- Refrigerator _____
- Range /oven _____
- Disposal _____
- Dishwasher _____
- Fan / hood _____
- Compactor _____
- Washer / dryer _____
- Microwave _____
- Intercom _____

Attic
- ☐ None
- ☐ Stairs
- ☐ Drop stair
- ☐ Scuttle
- ☐ Floor
- ☐ Heated
- ☐ Finished
- ☐ Unfinished

Car storage : ☐ Garage ☐ Attached ☐ Adequate ☐ None
No. cars : ☐ Carport ☐ Detached ☐ Inadequate ☐ Offstreet

Improvement analysis	Good	Avg.	Fair	Poor
Quality of construction	☐	☐	☐	☐
Condition of improvements	☐	☐	☐	☐
Room sizes / layout	☐	☐	☐	☐
Closets and storage	☐	☐	☐	☐
Energy efficiency	☐	☐	☐	☐
Plumbing - adequacy & condition	☐	☐	☐	☐
Electrical - adequacy & condition	☐	☐	☐	☐
Kitchen cabinets - adequacy & cond.	☐	☐	☐	☐
Compatibility to neighborhood	☐	☐	☐	☐
Appeal & marketability	☐	☐	☐	☐
Estimated remaining economic life				years

Comments on repairs needed, additional features, modernization, etc. : _____

Additional comments on neighborhood, site & description of improvements

Depreciation (physical, functional, and external inadequacies, etc.) : _____

Environmental conditions observed by or known to the appraiser : _____

VALUATION ANALYSIS

Purpose of Appraisal is to estimate Market Value as defined in the Certification & Statement of Limiting Conditions.

Cost approach

Comments on cost approach, accrued depreciation, and estimated site value : _____

ESTIMATED REPRODUCTION COST - NEW - OF IMPROVEMENTS :
- _____ Sq.Ft. @ $ _____ = $ _____
- _____ Sq.Ft. @ $ _____ = _____
- _____ Sq.Ft. @ $ _____ = _____
- _____ Sq.Ft. @ $ _____ = _____
- Extras _____ = _____
- _____ = _____
- _____ = _____
- Special Energy Efficient Items _____ = _____
- Porches, Patios, etc. _____ = _____
- Total Estimated Cost New . . . . = $ . . . . .

Less: Physical Functional External

Depreciation _____ = $ _____
Depreciated Value of Improvements . . . . = $ . . .
Site Imp. "as is" (driveway, landscaping, etc.) . . . . . = $ _____
ESTIMATED SITE VALUE . . . . = $ . . . .
(If leasehold, show only leasehold value.) . . . .
INDICATED VALUE BY COST APPROACH . . . . = $ _____

Freddie Mac Form 72\Fannie Mae Form 1025
—continued

Valuation
Analysis, continued   **SMALL RESIDENTIAL INCOME PROPERTY APPRAISAL REPORT**   File No.

Comparable rental data

At least three rental comparables should be reported and analyzed in this section.   The rental comparables should represent the most current rental information on properties as simi
proximate to the subject property as possible.   (This comparison is based on current rental data,   therefore, the rental comparables typically are not the same comparables used in
comparison analysis.) The appraisal report should assure the reader that the units and properties selected as comparables are comparable to the subject property (both the units and the
property) and accurately represent the rental market for the subject property   (unless otherwise stated within the report).

ITEM	SUBJECT	COMPARABLE RENTAL NO. 1	COMPARABLE RENTAL NO. 2	COMPARABLE RENTAL NO. 3
Address				
Proximity to subject				
Lease dates (if available)				
Rent survey date				
Data source				
Rent concessions				
Description of property - units, design, appeal, age, vacancies, and conditions	No.Units No.Vac. Yr. Blt.:	No.Units No.Vac. Yr.Blt.:	No.Units No.Vac. Yr.Blt.:	No.Units No.Vac. Yr.Blt.:

Individual unit breakdown	Rm. Count		Size	Rm. Count		Size	Total	Rm. Count		Size	Total	Rm. Count		Size	Total
	Tot	Br	Ba	Sq.Ft.	Tot	Br	Ba	Sq.Ft.	Monthly Rent	Tot	Br	Ba	Sq.Ft.	Monthly Rent	Tot	Br	Ba	Sq.Ft.	Monthly Rent

Utilities, furniture, and amenities included in rent				

Functional utility, basement, heating / cooling, project amenities, etc.				

Reconciliation of rental data and support for estimated market rents for the individual subject units (including the adjustments used, the adequacy of comparables, rental concessions,

Subject's rent schedule   The rent schedule reconciles the applicable indicated monthly market rents to the appropriate subject unit, and provides the estimated rents for the subject p
The appraiser must review the rent characteristics of the comparable sales to determine whether estimated rents should reflect actual or market rents.   For example, if actual
available on the sales comparables and used to derive the gross rent multiplier (GRM), actual rents for the subject should be used. If market rents were used to construct the comparable
and derive the GRM, market rents should be used.   The total gross estimated rent must represent rent characteristics consistent with the sales comparable data used to derive
The total gross estimated rent is not adjusted for vacancy.

Unit	Lease Date		No. Units Vacant	ACTUAL RENTS			ESTIMATED RENTS		
	Begin	End		Per Unit		Total Rents	Per Unit		Total Rents
				Unfurnished	Furnished		Unfurnished	Furnished	
				$	$	$	$	$	$
						$			$

Other monthly income (itemize)_____ $_____
Vacancy : Actual last year_____ % Previous year _____%   Estimated :_____% $_____ Annually   **Total gross estimated rent** $_____
Utilities included in estimated rents : ☐ Electric   ☐ Water   ☐ Sewer   ☐ Gas   ☐ Oil   ☐ Trash collection   ☐   _____

Comments on the rent schedule, actual rents, estimated rents (especially regarding differences between actual and estimated rents), utilities, etc. : _____

Freddie Mac Form 72 10/89   2-4 units   Page 3 of 4   Fannie Mae Form 1025 2-4 units   10/

Valuation
& Analysis, continued   **SMALL RESIDENTIAL INCOME PROPERTY APPRAISAL REPORT**   File No. _____

Sales comparison analysis

The undersigned has recited three recent sales of properties most similar & proximate to the subject property & has described & analyzed these in this analysis. If there is a significant between the subject & comparable properties, the analysis includes a dollar adjustment reflecting the market reaction to those items or an explanation supported by the market data. If cant item in the comparable property is superior to, or more favorable than, the subject property, a minus(-) adjustment is made, thus reducing the indicated value of subject; if a signifi in the comparable is inferior to, or less favorable than, the subject property, a plus(+) adjustment is made, thus increasing the indicated value of the subject. [(1) Sales Price/Gross Mont

ITEM	SUBJECT	COMPARABLE SALE NO. 1	COMPARABLE SALE NO. 2	COMPARABLE SALE NO. 3
Address				
Proximity to subject				
Sales price	$	☐Unf. ☐Furn. $	☐Unf. ☐Furn. $	☐Unf. ☐Furn. $
Sales price per GBA	$	$	$	$
Gross monthly rent	$	$	$	$
Gross mo. rent mult. (1)				
Sales price per unit	$	$	$	$
Sales price per room	$	$	$	$
Data source				

ADJUSTMENT	DESCRIPTION	DESCRIPTION	+/-$ Adjustment	DESCRIPTION	+/-$ Adjustment	DESCRIPTION	+/-$ Adjustment
Sales or financing concessions							
Date of sale / time							
Location							
Site / view							
Design and appeal							
Quality of construction							
Year built							
Condition							
Gross Building Area	Sq.ft.	Sq.ft.		Sq.ft.		Sq.ft.	

Unit breakdown

	No. of units	Rm. count Tot Br Ba	No. Vac.	No. of units	Rm. count Tot Br Ba	No. Vac.	No. of units	Rm. count Tot Br Ba	No. Vac.	No. of units	Rm. count Tot Br Ba	No. Vac.

Basement description							
Functional utility							
Heating / cooling							
Parking on / off site							
Project amenities and fee (If applicable)							
Other							
Net Adj. (total)		☐ + ☐ – $		☐ + ☐ – $		☐ + ☐ – $	
Adj. sales price of comparables			$		$		$

Comments on sales comparison (including reconciliation of all indicators of value as to consistency and relative strength and evaluation of the typical investors' / purchasers' motivati in that market.) : _____

_____

_____

       INDICATED VALUE BY SALES COMPARISON APPROACH $ _____

Analysis of any current agreement of sale, option, or listing of the subject property and analysis of any prior sales of subject and comparables within one year of the date of appraisal . _____

Income approach

Total gross monthly estimated rent $ _____ x gross rent multiplier (GRM) _____ = $ _____ INDICATED VALUE BY INCOME APPROAC

Comments on income approach (including expense ratios, if available, and reconciliation of the GRM) _____

_____

Reconciliation

INDICATED VALUE BY SALES COMPARISON APPROACH . . . . $ . . . .

INDICATED VALUE BY INCOME APPROACH . . . . $ . . . .

INDICATED VALUE BY COST APPROACH . . . . $ . . . .

This appraisal is made ☐ "as is" ☐ subject to the repairs, alterations, inspections or conditions listed below ☐ subject to completion per plans and specifications.

Comments and conditions of appraisal : _____

_____

Final reconciliation : _____

_____

_____

This appraisal is based upon the above conditions and the certification, contingent and limiting conditions, and Market Value definition that are stated in

Freddie Mac Form 439 / Fannie Mae Form 1004B (Rev. _____) ☐ attached or ☐ filed with client on _____ or ☐ other attached.

I (WE) ESTIMATE THE MARKET VALUE, AS DEFINED, OF THE SUBJECT PROPERTY AS OF _____ to be $ _____

I (We) certify that to the best of my (our) knowledge and belief the facts and data used herein are true and correct; that I (we) personally inspected the subject property, both inside and have personally made an exterior inspection of all comparables cited in this report; and that I (we) have no undisclosed interest, present or prospective therein.

APPRAISER(S)	REVIEW APPRAISER (if applicable)		
SIGNATURE	SIGNATURE	☐ Did	☐ Did not
NAME	NAME	inspect property	

Freddie Mac Form 72   10/89   2-4 units   Page 4 of 4   Fannie Mae Form 1025   2-4 units   10/

Freddie Mac Form 465\Fannie Mae Form 1073

APPRAISAL REPORT - INDIVIDUAL ☐ CONDOMINIUM OR ☐ PUD UNIT   File No. _____

NEIGHBORHOOD

Borrower _____ Census Tract _____ Map Reference _____
Unit No. _____ Address _____ Project Name/Phase No. _____
City _____ County _____ State _____ Zip Code _____
Actual Real Estate Taxes $ _____ (yr.) Sale Price $ _____ Property Rights Appraised ☐ Fee ☐ Leasehold
Loan charges to be paid by seller $ _____ Other sales concessions _____
Lender/Client _____ Lender's Address _____
Occupant _____ Appraiser _____ Instructions to Appraiser _____
☐ FNMA 1073A required   ☐ FHLMC 465 Addendum A required   ☐ FHLMC 465 Addendum B required

				NEIGHBORHOOD RATING	Good	Avg.	Fair	Poor
Location	☐ Urban	☐ Suburban	☐ Rural					
Built up	☐ Over 75%	☐ 25% to 75%	☐ Under 25%	Adequacy of Shopping	☐	☐	☐	☐
Growth Rate ☐ Fully Developed	☐ Rapid	☐ Steady	☐ Slow	Employment Opportunities	☐	☐	☐	☐
Property Values	☐ Increasing	☐ Stable	☐ Declining	Recreational Facilities	☐	☐	☐	☐
Demand/Supply	☐ Shortage	☐ In Balance	☐ Oversupply	Adequacy of Utilities	☐	☐	☐	☐
Marketing Time	☐ Under 3 Mos.	☐ 4-6 Mos.	☐ Over 6 Mos.	Property Compatibility	☐	☐	☐	☐

Present Land Use _____ % 1 Family _____ % 2-4 Family _____ % Apts _____ % Condo   Protection from Detrimental Conditions ☐ ☐ ☐ ☐
_____ % Commercial _____ % Industrial _____ % Vacant   Police and Fire Protection ☐ ☐ ☐ ☐
Change in Present Land Use ☐ Not Likely ☐ Likely ☐ Taking Place*   General Appearance of Properties ☐ ☐ ☐ ☐
*From _____ To _____   Appeal to Market ☐ ☐ ☐ ☐

Predominant Occupancy	☐ Owner	☐ Tenant	____ % Vacant		Distance	Access or Convenience
Condominium: Price Range $ ____ to $ ____ Predominant $ ____				Public Transportation		☐ ☐ ☐ ☐
Age ____ yrs. to ____ yrs. Predominant ____ yrs.				Employment Centers		☐ ☐ ☐ ☐
Single Family: Price Range $ ____ to $ ____ Predominant $ ____				Neighborhood Shopping		☐ ☐ ☐ ☐
Age ____ yrs. to ____ yrs. Predominant ____ yrs.				Grammar Schools		☐ ☐ ☐ ☐
Describe potential for additional Condo/PUD units in nearby area _____				Freeway Access		☐ ☐ ☐ ☐

Note: FHLMC/FNMA do not consider race or the racial composition of the neighborhood to be reliable appraisal factors.

Describe those factors, favorable or unfavorable, affecting marketability (e.g. public parks, schools, noise, view, mkt. area, population size, financial ability). _____

SITE

Lot Dimensions (if PUD) _____ = _____ Sq. Ft. ☐ Corner Lot   Project Density When Completed as Planned _____ Units/Acre
Zoning Classification _____   Present improvements ☐ do ☐ do not conform to zoning regulations
Highest and best use: ☐ Present use ☐ Other (specify) _____

	Public	Other (Describe)	OFF-SITE IMPROVEMENTS	Project Ingress/Egress (adequacy) _____
Elec.	☐		Street Access: ☐ Public ☐ Private	Topo _____
Gas	☐		Surface _____	Size/Shape _____
Water	☐		Maintenance: ☐ Public ☐ Private	View Amenity _____
San. Sewer	☐		☐ Storm Sewer ☐ Curb/Gutter	Drainage/Flood Conditions _____
	☐ Underground Elec. & Tel.		☐ Sidewalk ☐ Street Lights	Is the property in a HUD identified Special Flood Hazard Area? ☐ No ☐ Yes

Comments (including any easements, encroachments or other adverse conditions) _____

PROJECT IMPROVEMENTS

			PROJECT RATING	Good	Avg.	Fair	Poor
☐ Existing Approx. Year Built 19 ___ Original Use _____							
☐ Condo ☐ PUD	☐ Converted (19 ___)		Location	☐	☐	☐	☐
TYPE ☐ Proposed	☐ Under Construction		General Appearance	☐	☐	☐	☐
PROJECT ☐ Elevator	☐ Walk-up No. of Stories ___		Amenities and Recreational Facilities	☐	☐	☐	☐
☐ Row or Town House	☐ Other (specify) ___		Density (units per acre)	☐	☐	☐	☐
☐ Primary Residence	☐ Second Home or Recreational		Unit Mix	☐	☐	☐	☐
If Completed: No. Phases ___	No. Units ___	No. Sold ___	Quality of Constr. (mat'l & finish)	☐	☐	☐	☐
If Incomplete: Planned No. Phases ___	No. Units ___	No. Sold ___	Condition of Exterior	☐	☐	☐	☐
Units in Subject Phase: Total ___	Completed ___ Sold ___	Rented ___	Condition of Interior	☐	☐	☐	☐
Approx. No. Units for Sale: Subject Project ___	Subject Phase ___		Appeal to Market	☐	☐	☐	☐

Exterior Wall _____ Roof Covering _____ Security Features _____
Elevator: No. _____ Adequacy & Condition _____ Soundproofing: Vertical _____ Horizontal _____
Parking: Total No. Spaces _____ Ratio _____ Spaces/Unit _____ Type _____ No. Spaces of Guest Parking _____
Describe common elements or recreational facilities _____
Are any common elements, rec. facilities or parking leased to Owners Assoc.? _____ If yes, attach addendum describing rental, terms and options.

SUBJECT UNIT

☐ Existing ☐ Proposed ☐ Under Constr. Floor No. ___ Unit Livable Area ___ / Basement ___ % Finished ___ /
Parking for Unit: No. ___ Type ___ ☐ Assigned ☐ Owned Convenience to Unit _____

Room List	Foyer	Liv	Din	Kit	Bdrm	Bath	Fam	Rec	Lndry	Other	UNIT RATING	Good	Avg.	Fair	Poor
Basement											Condition of Improvement	☐	☐	☐	☐
1st Level											Room Sizes and Layout	☐	☐	☐	☐
2nd Level											Adequacy of Closets and Storage	☐	☐	☐	☐
											Kit. Equip., Cabinets & Workspace	☐	☐	☐	☐

Floors: ☐ Hardwood ☐ Carpet over _____   Plumbing - Adequacy and Condition ☐ ☐ ☐ ☐
Int. Walls ☐ Drywall ☐ Plaster _____   Electrical - Adequacy and Condition ☐ ☐ ☐ ☐
Trim/Finish: ☐ Good ☐ Average ☐ Fair ☐ Poor   Adequacy of Soundproofing ☐ ☐ ☐ ☐
Bath Floor: ☐ Ceramic _____ Wainscot ☐ Ceramic _____   Adequacy of Insulation ☐ ☐ ☐ ☐
Windows (type): _____ ☐ Storm Sash ☐ Screens ☐ Combo   Location within Project or View ☐ ☐ ☐ ☐
Kitchen Equip: ☐ Refrig. ☐ Range/Oven ☐ Fan/Hood ☐ Washer ☐ Dryer   Overall Livability ☐ ☐ ☐ ☐
☐ Intercom ☐ Disposal ☐ Dishwasher ☐ Microwave ☐ Compacter   Appeal and Marketability ☐ ☐ ☐ ☐
HEAT: Type _____ Fuel _____ Cond. _____   Est. Effective Age ___ to ___ yrs.
AIR COND: ☐ Central ☐ Other _____ ☐ Adequate ☐ Inadequate   Est. Remaining Economic Life ___ to ___ yrs.
☐ Earth sheltered Housing Design ☐ Solar Design/Landscape ☐ Solar Space Hear/Air Cond. ☐ Solar Hot Water
☐ Flue Damper ☐ Elec./Mech. Gas Furn. Ignition ☐ Auto Setback Thermostat ☐ Dble/Triple Glased Windows ☐ Caulk/Wheatherstrip
INSULATION (state R-Factor if known) ☐ Walls ___ ☐ Ceiling ___ ☐ Floor ___ ☐ Roof/Attic ___ ☐ Water Heater ___
If rehab proposed, do plans and specs provide for adequate energy conservation? _____ If no, attach description of modification needed.
ENERGY EFFICIENCY APPEARS: ☐ High ☐ Adequate ☐ Low   Energy Audit: ☐ Yes (attach, if available) ☐ No
COMMENTS (special features, functional or physical inadequacies, modernization or repair needed, etc.) _____

FHLMC Form 465 Rev. 9/80 12 CPI   ATTACH DESCRIPTIVE PHOTOGRAPHS OF SUBJECT PROPERTY AND STREET SCENE   FNMA Form 1073 Rev. 9/80

94

BUDGET ANALYSIS

Unit Charge $ _____ /Mo. x 12 = $ _____ /Yr. ($ _____ /Sq. Ft./year of livable area) Ground Rent (if any) $ _____ /yr.

Utilities included in unit charge: ☐ None ☐ Heat ☐ Air Cond. ☐ Electricity ☐ Gas ☐ Water ☐ Sewer

Note any fees, other than regular Condo/PUD charges, for use of facilities _____

To properly maintain the project and provide the services anticipated, the budget appears ☐ High ☐ Adequate ☐ Inadequate

Compared to other competitive projects of similar quality and design subject unit charge apears: ☐ High ☐ Reasonable ☐ Low

Management Group: ☐ Owners Association ☐ Developer ☐ Management Agent (identify)

Quality of Management and its enforcement of Rules and Regulations appears: ☐ Superior ☐ Good ☐ Adequate ☐ Inadequate

Special or unusual characteristics in the Condo/PUD Documents or otherwise known to the appraiser, that would affect marketability (if none, so state)

Comments

COST APPROACH

NOTE: FHLMC does not require the cost approach in the appraisal of condominium or PUD units.

Cost Approach (to be used only for detached, semi-detached, and town house units):

Reproduction Cost New _____ Sq. Ft. @ $ _____ per Sq. Ft. = ____ $ _____

Less Depreciation: Physical $ _____ Functional $ _____ Economic $ _____ (_____)

Depreciated Value of Improvements: _____

Add Land Value (if leasehold, show only leasehold value - attach calculations) _____

Pro-rata Share of Value of Amenities $ _____

Total Indicated Value: ☐ FEE SIMPLE ☐ LEASEHOLD $ _____

Comments regarding estimate of depreciation and value of land and amenity package _____

MARKET DATA ANALYSIS

The appraiser, whenever possible, should analyze two comparable sales from within the subject project. However, when appraising a unit in a new or newly converted project, at least two comparables should be selected from outside the subject project. In the following analysis, the comparable should always be adjusted to the subject unit and not vice versa. If a significant feature of the comparable is superior to the subject unit, a minus (-) adjustment should be made to the comparable; if such a feature of the comparable is inferior to the subject, a plus (+) adjustment should be made to the comparable.

LIST ONLY THOSE ITEMS THAT REQUIRE ADJUSTMENT

ITEM	Subject Property	COMPARABLE NO. 1		COMPARABLE NO. 2		COMPARABLE NO. 3	
Address-Unit No.							
Project Name							
Proximity to Subj.							
Sales Price	$	$		$		$	
Price/Living Area	$	$		$		$	
Data Source							
	DESCRIPTION	DESCRIPTION	Adjustment	DESCRIPTION	Adjustment	DESCRIPTION	Adjustment
Date of Sale and Time Adjustment							
Location							
Site/View							
Design and Appeal							
Quality of Constr.							
Age							
Condition							
Living Area, Room Count & Total	Total B-rms Baths	Total B-rms Baths		Total B-rms Baths		Total B-rms Baths	
Gross Living Area	Sq. Ft.	Sq. Ft.		Sq. Ft.		Sq. Ft.	
Basement & Bsmt. Finished Rooms							
Functional Utility							
Air Conditioning							
Storage							
Parking Facilities							
Common Elements and Recreation Facilities							
Mo. Assessment							
Leasehold/Fee							
Special Energy Efficient Items							
Other (e.g. fireplaces, kitchen equip., remodeling)							
Sales or Financing Concessions							
Net Adj. (total)		☐Plus ☐Minus	$	☐Plus ☐Minus	$	☐Plus ☐Minus	$
Indicated value of Subject			$		$		$

Comments on Market Data Analysis _____

INDICATED VALUE BY MARKET DATA APPROACH $ _____

INDICATED VALUE BY INCOME APPROACH (If applicable) Economic Market Rent $ _____ /Mo. x Gross Rent Multiplier _____ = $ _____

This appraisal is made ☐ "as is" ☐ subject to repairs, alterations, or conditions listed below ☐ subject to completion per plans and specifications.

Comments and Conditions of Appraisal: _____

Final Reconciliation: _____

Construction Warranty ☐ Yes ☐ No Name of Warranty Program _____ Warranty Coverage Expires _____

This appraisal is based upon the above requirements, the certification, contingent and limiting conditions, and Market Value definition that are stated in

☐ FHLMC Form 439 (Rev. 7/86)/FNMA Form 1004B (Rev. 7/86) filed with client _____ ,19____ ☐ attached.

I ESTIMATE THE MARKET VALUE, AS DEFINED OF SUBJECT PROPERTY AS OF _____ ,19____ to be $ _____

Appraiser(s) _____ Review Appraiser (if applicable) _____

Date Report Signed _____ ,19____ ☐ Did ☐ Did Not Physically Inspect Property

FHLMC Form 465 Rev. 9/80

FNMA Form 1073 Rev. 9/80

Employee Relocation Council
Residential Appraisal Report Form

**EMPLOYEE RELOCATION COUNCIL
RESIDENTIAL APPRAISAL REPORT**

E-R-C
is a non-profit membership
organization concerned with the
transfer of corporate employees.

Client File No.: _____
Homeowner: _____
_____
Address: _____
_____
Date: _____
Appraiser File No.: _____
Appraiser: _____

DEFINITIONS AND INSTRUCTIONS RELATING TO THE RELOCATION APPRAISAL

Purpose of the Relocation Appraisal:

To establish the most probable sales price for a relocated employee's primary residence, assuming an arm's length transaction.

Definition of the Relocation Appraisal:

The most probable sales price of a residential housing unit, using the market approach to value.

Definition of Market Data Approach to Value:

The price at which a property would most probably sell, "as is," if exposed to the market for a reasonable period of time, where payment is made in cash or its equivalent. Implicit in this definition is the consummation of the sale with passing of title from seller to buyer under conditions whereby:

1) Both parties are well informed and acting in what they consider their best interests.
2) A reasonable amount of time is allowed for exposure in the local market. A reasonable period is up to 120 days.
3) Financing, if any, is on terms generally available in the community and typical for the property type in its locale. (When the client has specifically requested consideration of special financing or an assumable loan, discuss its effect on the most probable sales price in the FINANCING section on Page 3.)
4) Forecasting is applied in making an estimate of a future happening or condition, based on an analysis of trends in the recent past, tempered with analytical judgment concerning the probable extent to which these trends will continue into the future, and reflecting an estimated impact, if any, upon the most probable sales price.

General Guidelines

The appraiser must observe the following general guidelines in determining the most probable sales price. The appraiser is to:

1) Estimate the most probable sales price considering the property "as is" on the date of inspection. "As is" should reflect the appearance of the subject property, as compared with similar properties in that market. Equal consideration should be given to both property condition and appeal (exterior/interior), with adjustments made to reflect market reaction to the property's appearance, from a buyer's point of view. The actual cost to cure may or may not be the appropriate measure for this adjustment. Rather, the client is looking for the contribution to value of the following items:
   a) Condition (e.g., modernization, restoration, repairs, necessary improvements, etc.); and
   b) Appeal (e.g., construction upgrades, custom decorating, personalized decor, etc.).
If there is a circumstance where the appraiser is unable to determine the "as is" condition (part a) for such situations as: in-process construction or improvements, suspected structural, water and/or roof related problems, etc., notify the client immediately.

2) Stress what the property should sell for in the current marketplace, giving particular attention to the analysis of comparable sales (or homes under contract), competitive listings, supply and demand, and overall market conditions. The appraiser should also consider and make necessary adjustments for other factors, such as: the residence's exposure to the market; availability and terms of financing; over-improvements; and location.

3) Reflect in your appraised value opinion, as of the date of the appraisal:
   a) An adjustment for any value that may have been created by comparable sale prices (or homes under contract) that were influenced by discount points paid by the seller or those comparables that were sold by loan assumption, installment contract, seller carry back, or any form of preferential financing. This also applies to situations where the seller pays certain buyer costs such as buy downs, fees, or credits. In these situations, adjustments should be noted and described for the specific comparable sale.

   b) The difference in discount points between those charged on the comparable sales (or homes under contract) and those charged currently, if it is the custom of lenders to charge discount points to sellers.

4) Develop the appraised value opinion, assuming the property is free and clear of all non-mortgage encumbrances, with the owner responsible for discharging all liens and unpaid installments of special assessments for improvements completed. If the special assessments are still pending and the improvements are not yet completed, the appraiser should include any additional value that may attribute to the pending improvements. If paying off an assessment provides the subject property with an advantage over the comparable sales and competitive listings, this should be reflected in the appraised value.

5) Gross Living Area (GLA) is the calculation of the total living area, expressed in square footage. This calculation is derived from exterior measurements (except condominiums and cooperatives), and is limited to the finished and habitable above-grade living area only. Basement areas (finished and unfinished) are not included in Gross Living Area, but may be a valuable and significant contribution, and should be calculated and shown separately in the IMPROVEMENTS and MARKET DATA ANALYSIS sections of the report.

6) The NEIGHBORHOOD, PROPERTY RATING, and MARKET DATA ANALYSIS sections of this appraisal report require use of the terms "Good", "Average", "Fair", or "Poor" to describe the subject property and the comparable sales. When rating the various attributes of the subject property and neighborhood, compare the characteristics to those for competing properties and neighborhoods. (e.g., A luxury, custom-designed home may be rated "average" as compared with competitive properties that also are luxury, custom-designed homes.) The ratings are defined as follows:

☐ Good: the amenity or characteristic is superior to the same characteristic found in competing properties and neighborhoods;
☐ Average: the amenity or characteristic is equal to the same characteristic found in competing properties and neighborhoods;
☐ Fair: the amenity or characteristic is inferior to the same characteristic found in competing properties and neighborhoods; or
☐ Poor: the amenity or characteristic is infrequently seen or does not exist, but is found in competing properties and neighborhoods.

© Copyright 1991, Employee Relocation Council

ERC-3 Rev. 1/91

Procedural Guidelines

In addition to the aforementioned general guidelines, the appraiser must be aware of and follow these specific guidelines:

1. Appraisers are frequently the sole visible representative of the client to the relocated homeowner. Therefore, a professional and courteous manner should be presented.

2. When an appraiser assignment is directed to a specific individual, that appraiser must personally inspect the property and complete the assignment unless approval for a substitution is obtained from the client.

3. On the day the appraiser is contacted with the appraisal request, contact should be made with the employee (or spouse) for an appointment. If the employee (or spouse) cannot be reached on the same day, let the client know so they can assist in locating the homeowner.

4. Inspect the property within two working days and contact the client with the verbal figure within four working days of the original request (unless the transferring employee delays the process). If the appraisal cannot be completed in the required time frame, or if the appraiser will be unavailable to discuss the assignment after completion, the assignment should not be accepted.

5. If access to the property cannot be gained, if valuation problems arise, or if an inspection is required for clarification (such as a structural engineer's report, etc.), the client should be called immediately.

6. Completed copies of the typewritten appraisal report should be mailed within seven working days of the original request (providing there are not delays created by the homeowner).

7. Sufficient time should be taken when inspecting the subject property to impart confidence to the homeowner even if the appraiser is familiar with the property.

8. Consider any information that the homeowner feels is important to the value of his/her home.

9. The appraiser should not discuss his/her appraisal opinions or reveal sensitive information to anyone other than the client. If the homeowner (or spouse) asks general questions as it relates to the appraisal process, feel free to discuss generalities.

10. The appraiser who arrives at the homeowner's property while another appraiser or broker is present, should leave the property immediately and reschedule the appointment.

11. An appraiser will not accept an appraisal assignment if there is a conflict of interest such as: recently appraising the house for another party, an association with the listing agent/company, etc.

12. Appraisers will not solicit a listing or generate a referral as a result of an appraisal assignment.

13. Call the client to clarify the instructions if they are not completely understood.

14. Include the following exhibits:
   a. Photos of the front and rear view of the residence, street scene of the property, factors in near-by vicinity which affect subject property, either favorably or adversely.
   b. Photos of all comparables. (Please attach all photos separately.)
   c. Sketch of the floor plan of subject property (not necessarily to scale).
   d. Sketch of plot plan showing all improvements (not necessarily to scale).
   e. Map of the subdivision or area depicting locations of the subject, comparable sold properties and competitive listings.

Building Sketch (if grid is inadequate, please attach separate grid)

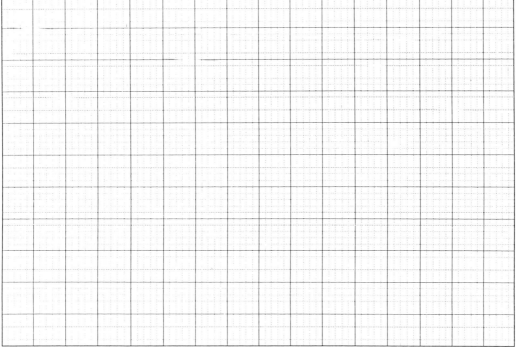

EMPLOYEE RELOCATION COUNCIL
RESIDENTIAL APPRAISAL REPORT

SUBJECT INFORMATION

Homeowner: _____ Occupant: ☐ homeowner ☐ tenant ☐ vacant

Property Address: _____ County: _____

City/State/Zip + 4: _____

Legal Description: _____

Property Rights Appraised: ☐ Fee ☒ PUD ☒ * Condominium ☐ Leasehold

Client/Contact: _____ File No.: _____

Address: _____

Appraiser: _____ File No. _____ Ph. # ( )

Address: _____

Is the subject property currently listed? ☐ Yes ☐ No Current List Price: $ _____ Agent: _____

Listing Company: _____ Ph. # ( )

Listing Co./Address: _____

FINANCING

Has the client specifically requested that you consider special financing or an assumable loan in the Most Probable Sales Price? ☐ Yes ☐ No

If yes, note who verified this information and describe which type (special financing or an assumption), its terms, and discuss its impact on potential purchasers and how it compares with the competing listings. _____

Describe current financing and typically available interest rates and terms. _____

TAXES & ASSESSMENTS

What are the actual real estate taxes? _____ Period covered from _____ to _____

Are taxes typical for the area and price range? ☐ Yes ☐ No If no, explain: _____

List any special assessments (including municipal, Homeowner Association dues, etc.) or additional encumbrances/liens (existing or pending). _____

NEIGHBORHOOD

					Good	Avg.	Fair	Poor
Location	☐ Urban	☐ Suburban	☐ Rural					
Built Up	☐ Over 75%	☐ 25% to 75%	☐ Under 25%	Employment Stability	☐	☐	☐	☐
Growth Rate ☐ Fully Dev.	☐ Rapid	☐ Steady	☐ Slow	Convenience to Employment	☐	☐	☐	☐
Property Values	☐ Increasing	☐ Stable	☐ Declining	Convenience to Shopping	☐	☐	☐	☐
Demand/Supply	☐ Shortage	☐ In Balance	☐ Over Supply	Convenience to Schools	☐	☐	☐	☐
Marketing Time	☐ Up to 120 Days	☐ 121 to 180 Days	☐ Over 180 Days	Adequacy of Public Trans.	☐	☐	☐	☐
Present Land Use ___ % 1 Family ___ % 2-4 Family ___ % Apts. ___ % Condo				Recreational Facilities	☐	☐	☐	☐
___ % Commercial ___ % Industrial ___ % Vacant ___ %				Adequacy of Utilities	☐	☐	☐	☐
Change in Present Land Use	☐ Not Likely	☐ Likely (*)	☐ Taking Place (*)	Property Compatibility	☐	☐	☐	☐
(*) From _____ To _____				Protection from Detrimental Conds.	☐	☐	☐	☐
Predominant Occupancy	☐ Owner	☐ Tenant	___ % Vacant	Police and Fire Protection	☐	☐	☐	☐
S. Fam. Price Range $ ___ to $ ___ Predominant Value $ ___				General Appearance of Properties	☐	☐	☐	☐
Single Family Age ___ Yrs. to ___ Yrs. Predominant Age ___ Yrs.				Appeal to Market				

New Construction Activity ☐ Yes ☐ No If yes, are incentives offered? ☐ Yes ☐ No   REO Competition? ☐ Yes ☐ No

Comment on the immediate neighborhood including all factors, favorable or unfavorable, affecting the subject's marketability (e.g., public parks, schools, view, external obsolescence). _____

SITE

Dimensions _____ = _____ Sq. Ft. or Acres ☐ Corner Lot

Zoning Classification _____ Present Improvements ☐ do ☐ do not conform to zoning regulations.

Highest and Best Use ☐ Present Use ☐ Other (specify) _____

	Public	Other (Describe)	OFF-SITE IMPROVEMENTS		Topo _____
Electric	☐		Street Access:	☐ Public ☐ Private	Size _____
Gas	☐		Surface		Shape _____
Water	☐		Maintenance:	☐ Public ☐ Private	View _____
San. Sewer	☐		☐ Storm Sewer	☐ Curb/Gutter	Drainage _____
	☐ Undergrnd. Elect. & Tel.		☐ Sidewalk	☐ Street Lights	

Is the property located in a HUD Identified Special Flood Hazard Area? ☐ No ☐ Yes

Is the property size atypical for the area? ☐ Yes ☐ No If atypical, (e.g. excess acreage, multiple parcels) explain in the comment section below.

Comments (favorable or unfavorable, including any apparent adverse easements, encroachments or other adverse conditions) _____

* If condominium is checked, ask client if the E-R-C Condominium Addendum should be used to supplement this report.

© Copyright 1991, Employee Relocation Council

ERC-3 Rev. 1/91

EMPLOYEE RELOCATION COUNCIL
RESIDENTIAL APPRAISAL REPORT

IMPROVEMENTS

☐ Existing Const.   ☐ Under Const.   No. Units _____   Type (det., duplex, semi/det., etc.) _____   Design (Colonial, split level, etc.) _____   Exterior Walls _____

Yrs. Actual _____ Effective _____ to _____   No. Stories _____

Roof Material _____   Gutters and Downspouts ☐ NONE   Window (Type): _____   Insulation ☐ None ☐ Floor

☐ Storm Sash   ☐ Screens   ☐ Combo.   ☐ Ceiling ☐ Roof ☐ Wall

☐ Manufactured Housing   **BSMT.** Bsmt. Area _____ Sq. Ft. _____ % Finished   Finished Ceiling _____

Foundation Walls _____   ☐ Outside Entrance   ☐ Sump Pump   Finished Walls _____

☐ Concrete Floor   ☐ Floor Drain   Finished Floor _____

☐ Slab on Grade   ☐ Crawl Space   Evidence of: ☐ Dampness   ☐ Termites   ☐ Structural Settlement: _____

List any required inspections (e.g., municipal, state, certificate of occupancy, federal, etc.). _____

List any recommended inspections and why (e.g., structural, mechanical, roof, etc.). _____

Has the owner secured the necessary permits for all additions and improvements?   ☐ Yes   ☐ No

How was this verified? _____

Construction Warranty ☐ Yes ☐ No   Name of Warranty Program _____   Waranty Coverage Expires _____

If yes, is it transferable? ☐ Yes ☐ No

ROOM LIST

Room List	Foyer	Living	Dining	Kitchen	Den	Family Rm.	Rec. Room	Bedrooms	No. Baths	Laundry	Other
Basement											
1st Level											
2nd Level											

Total finished and habitable area above grade contains: _____ rooms _____ bedrooms _____ baths. Gross Living Area _____ Sq. Ft.

INTERIOR FINISH AND EQUIPMENT

Kitchen Equipment: ☐ Refrigerator ☐ Range/Oven ☐ Micro-wave ☐ Dishwasher ☐ Fan/Hood ☐ Compact ☐ Disposal ☐ Other _____

HEAT: Type _____ Fuel _____ Cond. _____ AIR COND. ☐ Central ☐ Other ☐ Adequate ☐ Inadequate

Floors	☐ Hardwood	☐ Carpet Over	☐ _____	_____
Walls	☐ Drywall	☐ Plaster	☐	
Trim/Finish	☐ Good	☐ Average	☐ Fair ☐ Poor	
Bath Floor	☐ Ceramic	☐		
Bath Wainscot	☐ Ceramic	☐ _____		

Energy related (including energy efficient items) _____

PROPERTY RATING

Comment on Good and/or Poor Ratings.	Good	Avg.	Fair	Poor
Quality of Construction (Materials & Finish)	☐	☐	☐	☐
Condition of Improvements	☐	☐	☐	☐
Room Sizes and Layout	☐	☐	☐	☐
Closets and Storage	☐	☐	☐	☐
Insulation - Adequacy	☐	☐	☐	☐
Plumbing - Adequacy and Condition	☐	☐	☐	☐
Electrical - Adequacy and Condition	☐	☐	☐	☐
Compatibility to Neighborhood	☐	☐	☐	☐
Overall Livability	☐	☐	☐	☐
Appeal and Marketability	☐	☐	☐	☐

ATTIC: ☐ Yes ☐ No ☐ Stairway ☐ Drop-Stair ☐ Scuttle ☐ Floored ☐ Heated

Finished (Describe) _____

Car Storage ☐ Garage ☐ Blt. In ☐ Attached ☐ Detached ☐ Car Port

No. Cars # _____ ☐ Adequate ☐ Inadequate   Condition: _____

SPECIAL FEATURES

Specifically describe any special features which affect the appraised value of the subject property such as upgrades, additions, improvements, etc. _____

AS IS CONDITION/APPEAL

As required in paragraph 1 of the General Guidelines relative to "as is" *condition and appeal,* list any physical inadequacies, functional obsolescence, repairs, or cosmetic improvements you recommend that would put the home in a competitive marketable condition. Estimate the cost of each recommended repair/improvement. Furnish photographs if warranted.

PERSONAL PROPERTY

Note all personal property included in most probable sales price. How was this verified: _____

ERC-3 Rev. 1/91

EMPLOYEE RELOCATION COUNCIL
RESIDENTIAL APPRAISAL REPORT

ITEM	SUBJECT			LISTING # 1			LISTING # 2			LISTING # 3		
Address												
Proximity to Subj./Location												
Original List Price												
Current List Price												
Last Price Revision Date												
Days-on-Market												
Site/View												
Design & Style												
Age												
Condition												
Above Grade Room Count	Tot:	B-rms.	Ba.	Tot:	B-rms.	Ba.	Tot:	B-rms.	Ba.	Tot:	B-rms.	Ba.
Approx. Gross Living Area			sq. ft.			sq. ft.			sq. ft.			sq. ft.
Basement Area												
Car Storage												
Other (e.g. special/financing concessions, amenities, etc.)												

COMPETING LISTINGS

Describe the value-related differences between the subject property and the competing listings (including *financing, terms, condition, location, appeal, deferred maintenance, utility, style, view, days-on-market, and other amenities*). Are seller financing, discount points, and/or other seller concessions being offered? *If yes, explain below.*

Listing # 1 _____

Listing # 2 _____

Listing # 3 _____

MARKET CONDITIONS

Describe current supply/demand characteristics in the subject marketing area (e.g.: new construction, number of competing listings) and other pertinent market issues. _____

Describe forecasted market/economic trends and their anticipated impact on marketing the subject property. _____

ADDITIONAL COMMENTS

EMPLOYEE RELOCATION COUNCIL
RESIDENTIAL APPRAISAL REPORT

The appraiser has analyzed those sales considered to be most representative of the subject property. The following descriptions include a dollar adjustment, reflecting market reaction to those items of significant variation between the subject and comparable properties. If a significant item in the comparable property is superior to, or more favorable than, the subject property, a minus (-) adjustment is made, thus reducing the indicated value of subject; if a significant item in the comparable is inferior to, or less favorable than, the subject property, a plus (+) adjustment is made, thus increasing the indicated value of the subject. See General Guideline Number 6 for definitions of good, average, fair, and poor.

ITEM	SUBJECT	COMPARABLE #1		COMPARABLE #2		COMPARABLE #3	
Address							
Proximity to Subj.							
Sales Price		$		$		$	
Closing Date							
Data Source							
Market Change:	DESCRIPTION	DESCRIPTION	+(-)$ Adjustment	DESCRIPTION	+(-)$ Adjustment	DESCRIPTION	+(-)$ Adjustment
Contract to Inspection Date							
Sales or Financing Concessions							
Location							
Site/View							
Ext. Design/Appeal							
Quality of Const.							
Age							
Condition							
Int. Appeal/Decor							
Total Rooms Above Grade And Gross Living Area (GLA)	Rms / B-rms / Baths: / sq. ft.	Rms / B-rms / Baths: / sq. ft.		Rms / B-rms / Baths: / sq. ft.		Rms / B-rms / Baths: / sq. ft.	
Basement Area							
Finished Rooms							
Functional Utility							
Air Conditioning							
Car Storage							
Decks, Patios							
Pools, etc.							
Special Features (e.g. energy related items, fireplace, kitchen remodeling, etc.)							
Other							
Forecasting							
Net Adj. (Total)		Plus / Minus $		Plus / Minus $		Plus / Minus $	
Adjusted Sales Price		$		$		$	
Describe Other							

MARKET DATA ANALYSIS

Discuss the most significant value-related differences between the subject property and the individual comparables, including but not limited to *financing, terms, condition, location, interior and exterior appeal, deferred maintenance, utility, style, view, days-on-market, and other amenities.*

Comparable Sale #1 _____

_____

_____

_____

_____

Comparable Sale #2 _____

_____

_____

_____

_____

Comparable Sale #3 _____

_____

_____

_____

Market Data Reconciliation: _____

_____

_____

_____

_____

_____

_____

I certify that I have personally inspected both the exterior and interior of the foregoing described property, and I have no interest in such, either present or contemplated. I further certify that I have adhered to the terms of the assignment as set forth in the definitions and instructions on page 1 of 6. (If more than one appraiser is involved in this assignment, including inspection and review, two signatures are required.) Most Probable Sales Price for the subject property based on the aforementioned certification is. . . . . $_____

CERTIFICATION

Appraiser(s) Signature: _____

Appraiser(s) (please type): _____ Date: _____

Review Appraiser(s) Signature (if applicable): _____

Review Appraiser(s) (if applicable please type): _____ Date: _____

Tax I.D. Number: _____

Homeowner: _____ Client File No.: _____

ERC-3 Rev. 1/91

Guide Note 2
Cash Equivalency in Value Estimates
in Accordance with Standards Rule 1-2 (b)

Introduction

An appraiser may be requested to estimate the value of real property on the assumption that certain specific financing is available from or through the seller that differs from the financing that is currently available from conventional lenders. Such an assumption as to financing may have no effect or may have a favorable or an unfavorable influence on the resulting estimate of value. Further, the sales data that is used in the sales comparison approach may have been affected by financing that influenced the price either favorably or unfavorably.

For several decades, real estate financing secured from institutional lenders had fairly consistent interest rates and terms and was often referred to as "typical" financing. The sale prices of property purchased with such "typical" financing were generally considered to be cash equivalent. However, high mortgage interest rates have prompted the use of alternative methods of financing. This so called "creative" financing included special incentives, interest buydowns, lender participation in income and equity, and other techniques. In addition, interest rate restrictions on government -guaranteed financing sometimes led to sellers paying the loan origination costs (points) for buyers and adjusting the sale price of the property to offset this added cost. This market condition introduced a myriad of complex terms and inducements that can have either a positive or negative impact on the price paid for a real property interest. As a result, "typical" financing took on a different meaning. What is typical today can be the methods and terms of financing that are prevalent in a specific geographic area or the dominant type of financing available to a particular type of property, either new or existing. The sale prices of property purchased under such terms may or may not be cash equivalent.

The requirement that appraisers analyze and measure the effect of financing is determined not by the availability of the particular financing but, rather, by its effect on the price of comparable sales and the price that most probably represents the defined value of the property being appraised.

In responding to the questions posed by the client that initiated the appraisal assignment, the appraiser must adhere to ethical standards and fundamental appraisal principles and practices that are sensitive to the market. A clear understanding is necessary between the appraiser and the client as to the interest being valued and the need for the appraiser to analyze existing, available and/or proposed financing. If the appraisal assignment is to estimate market value, the definition of market value must not only be consistent with the client's needs but must also meet the requirements of Standards Rule 1-2(b).

Basis for Proper Evaluation

The market value of a clearly identified property interest may be reported in a number of ways: (1) cash, (2) terms equivalent to cash, or (3) other precisely defined terms. An example of such other terms is the cash value of the equity interest subject to existing or proposed financing.

Adopted by the Board of Directors and effective January 1, 1991.

Standards Rule 1-2(b) requires an appraiser to clearly define the terms of such financing and estimate the effect of any financing, if any, on the value reported. Further, the market data supporting the valuation estimate must be described and explained. When submarket financing or financing with unusual conditions or incentives is involved and results in an effect on the estimate, the appraiser can either:

Report two values (as financed and cash equivalent); or

Report one value and indicate the positive or negative influence the financing terms have on the value reported.

Standards Rule 1-2(b) contains this reporting requirement so that interested parties will be aware of how much the favorable or unfavorable financing impacts the value reported. Standards Rule 1-2(b) does not imply that different terms of payment will always lead to a different value. It simply requires that the proper analysis be made and that an appropriate statement be included in the report.

Once a property owner finances the property, ownership becomes subject to the terms of the mortgage. The sum of the value of owner equity and the face amount of the balance(s) of the mortgage(s) may or may not be equal to the free and clear value of the property. Any difference represents the impact that the financing has on the value as indicated by the market (absent other factors that would impact value).

The same analysis outlined above must also be applied to comparable sales data. The appraiser should ascertain the terms of the financing involved in the acquisition of a comparable property and estimate the influence of such financing, if any, on the sale price. For example, does an all-cash sale differ from a sale in which the buyer assumed existing financing or secured new financing from the seller, a third party, or both? If so, why and what is the impact on price?

A clear distinction must be made between sale prices that are not affected by financing or other considerations, including sale prices for terms considered by the seller to be equivalent to cash transactions, and sales involving premiums or discounts due to financing. If the financing is unfavorable to the purchaser, one way that the difference may be measured is by the cost to retire the debt. Furthermore, the effect of financing on each comparable sale must be considered in light of the market as of the date of the sale, not the date of valuation of the subject. The appraiser should attempt to determine whether or not, at the time of sale, the financing affected the sale price in the minds of the parties to the transaction. If it did, the effect must be analyzed and an adjustment must be made and reported.

In estimating the value of a property, the appraiser must ascertain whether or not any existing financing is assumable, retirable, or replaceable. Also, the appraiser must estimate the potential value impact of the cost of items such as finders fees, points and prepayment penalties and the effect of the present worth of participations by lenders, if any. The appraiser should also judge the duration of any favorable or unfavorable influence from mortgages or participations. It should not be assumed that the benefit or detriment due to financing will continue throughout the stated amortization or participation terms. The value contribution of a mortgage fluctuates as interest rates rise and fall. The possibility of retiring unfavorable financing prior to its full payout period should also be considered.

The value of a property on the basis of cash or cash equivalency can be estimated most directly by comparing it with similar properties that were being sold for cash or its equivalent on the open market. However, if the total consideration for a comparable sale includes something other than cash (e.g., the exchange of property, life tenancy, or other interests), such consideration should be converted to cash equivalency. The concept of estimating cash equivalency goes beyond the discounting of debt encumbrances.

If sufficient data to permit a direct market comparison is not available, the cash equivalency of existing or proposed financing can be estimated by discounting the contractual terms at current market rates or yield rates for the same type of property and loan term over the expected holding period of the property. However, such mathematical methods should be weighed against other market indications.

In summary, demonstrated knowledge of the market financing available to the subject and comparable sale properties, analytical judgment, and common sense are required of the appraiser in determining whether or not specified financing impacts the value of a property. Standards Rule 1-2(b) requires that the impact of favorable or unfavorable financing on market value be estimated and reported. The value reported must be clear and meaningful to the client and cannot be misleading to the public or third parties.

Unacceptable Practices

1. Failure to accurately report the specific terms of any existing or proposed financing of the subject property, when such financing has an impact on the appraisal problem. (See S.R. 1-2(b)).

2. Failure to estimate and report the effect of favorable or unfavorable financing terms on value. (See S.R. 1-2(b)).

3. Failure to analyze and make appropriate adjustments to a comparable sale that included favorable or unfavorable financing terms as of the date of sale, when comparing the sale to the property being appraised. (See 1-2(b)).

4. Failure to state that financing data on a comparable sale is not available despite diligent investigation, and that reliance on the particular sale is thus limited. (See 1-4(b)(iii)).

(Please Note: Guide Notes to the Standards of Professional Appraisal Practice are an integral part of the Standards document. Guide Notes illustrate how the requirements of the Standards should be applied in various situations. Guide Notes should not be considered without referring to the appropriate Standards Rules.)

Guide Note 3
The Use of Form Appraisal Reports for Residential Property

Introduction

Most residential appraisal assignments require a report of findings on one of the approved forms used extensively in the secondary mortgage market. Examples are:

FHLMC 70/FNMA 1004 - Residential Appraisal Report

FHLMC 72 (2-12 units)/FNMA 1025 (2-4 units) - Small Residential Income Property

FHLMC 465/FNMA 1073 - Individual Condominium or PUD Unit

Many forms used by other entities are similar to the FHLMC/ FNMA forms. For example, the Employee Relocation Council (ERC) form, widely adopted by the employee relocation industry, is modeled after FNMA 1004 and the neighborhood, site, improvement descriptions, and market data analysis sections are nearly identical. However, other sections address specific interests of the client. Appraisers using the ERC form should be aware that its stated definition of market value varies somewhat from the definition adopted by FNMA. The ERC definition is somewhat generic and various companies hiring appraisers have adopted different interpretations of the market value definition in the ERC form. In addition, the ERC form does not include certifications that meet the requirements of the Appraisal Institute's Code of Professional Ethics and Standards of Professional Appraisal Practice. Other appraisal forms also have this deficiency.

It is the responsibility of the appraiser to obtain a clear understanding of the client's needs and to respond by applying fundamental appraisal principles and practices in an ethical manner. If a proposed appraisal assignment cannot be completed in accordance with the requirements of the Code of Professional Ethics and Standards of Professional Appraisal Practice, the assignment must not be accepted.

The move toward the use of common appraisal forms in the national marketplace has led to a greater uniformity in reports, but has not eliminated the difference in quality among reports. For this reason, guidelines for preparing form residential appraisal reports in accordance with the Standards of Professional Appraisal Practice are essential.

Basis for Proper Valuation

When using any form report, or signing the report as review appraiser, it is the responsibility of the appraiser and the review appraiser to ensure that the appropriate methods and techniques have been properly employed. Appropriate addenda must be added when additional information is required to complete the appraisal process. Such addenda are frequently used for value definition, certification, limiting conditions, maps, sketches, legal descriptions, and additional comments. When signing a report as

Adopted by the Board of Directors and effective January 1, 1991.

review appraiser, the appraiser accepts full responsibility for the contents of the report (cf. Explanatory Comment S.R. 2-5).

The appraiser must select the valuation methodology that is appropriate for each specific appraisal problem. The sales comparison approach is generally considered most relevant for residential property appraisals. Therefore, most forms are focused on the sales comparison approach and additional information may need to be added when the cost approach or the income capitalization approach are relevant to the subject property.

Whether or not the cost approach is developed, an estimate of the value contribution of land to overall value is usually required for the underwriting analyses employed in the secondary market.

Consistency is of paramount importance in form reports. The column labeled "Average" in the rating grid means "Typical" and does not have a negative connotation. A "Fair" or "Poor" rating for an item always requires a comment regarding any resulting effect on value. No items on the form should be left blank. If a category on the form is inappropriate for the specific appraisal problem, the item should be marked "Not Applicable." For example, public transportation in a rural location should be marked "Not Applicable" and not marked "Poor" or left blank.

The headings down the left side of the principal forms mirror the appraisal process. Care should be taken to relate the comments in these sections to the proper headings (e.g., site comments should not appear under the neighborhood section). If the value of the property being appraised does not fall within the typical price ranges identified in the neighborhood section, an adequate explanation must be provided. In completing the neighborhood rating grid, the subject neighborhood should be compared with other competing neighborhoods. In completing the property rating grid, the property should be compared with other properties within the subject neighborhood.

Highest and best use appears on most forms merely as a box to be checked because the use of the form itself is a statement of highest and best use. It is inappropriate to use a single-family dwelling report form if the appraiser concludes that the highest and best use of the property is a different use.

To ensure consistency, the description of the subject property in the adjustment grid of the sales comparison (market data) approach section of the form should be completed simultaneously with or checked carefully against the property description on the front of the form. Also, the effective age/remaining economic life estimates in the description of the improvements should be consistent with any accrued depreciation noted in the cost approach. The area of the basement (if any) and the percent of finished basement (if any), should be clearly stated.

The sales comparison (market data) approach section of the principal forms provides grids for the description and adjustment of three comparable sales. The appropriateness of the adjustments used is best demonstrated by bracketing the characteristics of the subject in selecting the sales data. The appraiser must decide whether additional sales or comments are necessary.

The term "Typical" should not be used in the "Description" column unless the report clearly identifies that which is typical in the market for the subject and sale properties. This is particularly important when considering an adjustment for "Sales or Financing Concessions" (cf: Guide Note 2). The appraiser should be aware that, although no adjustment among several types of prevailing financing options may be appropriate in the local market, underwriters in the secondary market are often the ultimate readers and reviewers of form reports and may not be familiar with the local markets of the properties comprising the loan package being considered for purchase. The appraiser's responsibility is to present the facts of each sale transaction in such a way that the reader or reviewer of the report, including the underwriter in the secondary market, will clearly understand the terms and conditions under which the subject is valued.

Unacceptable Practices

Many of the above comments describe recommended practices in contrast to unacceptable practices. Some additional unacceptable practices are:

1. Failure to consider the purpose, definitions, assumptions, conditions, and limitations that are inherent in the form report used for a residential appraisal. (See S.R. 1-2 (a)).

2. Failure to qualify a report or to refuse an assignment when underwriting criteria conflict with proper appraisal practice. The Departure Provision must be carefully considered when accepting such an appraisal assignment.

3. Signing an appraisal report as a review appraiser without setting forth the results of the review process or accepting full responsibility for the contents of the report. (See S.R. 2-5 and Standard 3).

4. Failure to consider, analyze and report any prior sales of the property being appraised within one year of the date of the appraisal (See S.R. 1-5(b)(i)).

(Please Note: Guide Notes to the Standards of Professional Appraisal Practice are an integral part of the Standards document. Guide Notes illustrate how the requirements of the Standards should be applied in various situations. Guide Notes should not be considered without referring to the appropriate Standards Rules.)

Guide Note 8
The Consideration of Hazardous Substances in the Appraisal Process

Introduction

The consideration of environmental forces along with social, economic and governmental forces is fundamental to the appraisal of real estate. Although appraisal literature has long recognized environmental forces as major determinants of value, the focus has been on the consideration of climatic conditions, topography and soil, the surrounding neighborhood, accessibility, and proximity to points of attraction. These environmental forces are readily apparent to a member of the general public who is not specifically trained as an expert in observing these forces. There is, however, a growing need to give special consideration to the impact of hazardous substances on the valuation of real property.

The growing need to consider hazardous substances is a recent trend stemming from the creation and identification of new hazards, recent federal and state legislation enacted to control and place responsibility for these hazards and an increasing public awareness of the problems resulting from these hazards.

The presence of hazardous substances on a property can significantly impact value. In some cases the property may have a "negative" value as the clean-up cost could be greater than the property value after clean up.

For the purpose of this guide note the term "hazardous substances" covers any material within, around or near a property that may have a negative effect on its value. Accordingly, the principles discussed in this guide note apply equally to hazards that may be contained within the property such as friable asbestos and external hazards such as toxic waste or contaminated ground water.

The purpose of this guide note is to provide guidance in the application of the Standards of Professional Appraisal Practice to the appraisal of real estate affected by hazardous substances and, in particular, to the consideration of such hazards in the appraisal process. It is not the purpose of this guide note to provide technical instructions or explanations concerning the detection or measurement of hazardous substances.

Basis for Proper Evaluation

The Competency Provision of the Uniform Standards of Professional Appraisal Practice requires the appraiser to either (1) have the knowledge and experience necessary to complete a specific appraisal assignment competently or (2) disclose the appraiser's lack of knowledge or experience to the client and take all steps necessary or appropriate to complete the assignment competently.

The Competency Provision is of particular importance in the appraisal of real property that may be affected by hazardous substances. The typical appraiser does not have the knowledge or experience required to detect the presence of hazardous substances or to measure the quantities of such material. The appraiser, like the buyers

Adopted by the Board of Directors and effective January 1, 1991.

and sellers in the open market, typically relies on the advice of others in matters that require special expertise.

There is nothing to prevent a professional appraiser from becoming an expert in other fields, but the typical real estate appraiser is neither required, nor expected, to be an expert in the special field of hazardous substances. This guide note therefore addresses the problem of hazardous substances from the viewpoint of the typical appraiser who is not qualified to detect or measure hazardous materials.

For an appraisal which accounts for the effects on value of hazardous substances, the typical appraiser would require the professional assistance of others. For an appraisal with no separate accounting for the possible effects on value of known hazardous substances, the typical appraiser would not require the professional assistance of others. These alternatives are further discussed below.

The appraiser may accept an assignment involving the consideration of hazardous substances without having the required knowledge and experience in this special field, provided the appraiser discloses such lack of knowledge and experience to the client prior to acceptance of the assignment and arranges to complete the assignment competently. This may require association with others who possess the required knowledge and experience or reliance on professional reports prepared by others who are reasonably believed to have the necessary knowledge and experience. If the appraiser draws conclusions based upon the advice or findings of others, the appraiser must believe that the advice or findings are made by persons who are licensed, certified or otherwise properly qualified. (See Guide Note 6, Reliance on Information or Reports Prepared by Others.) It is suggested that the client choose and hire any qualified environmental professionals.

In developing an appraisal based in part on the findings of others with respect to the existence of, and the effects of, hazardous substances, the appraiser must correctly employ those recognized methods and techniques that are necessary to produce a credible appraisal. The loss of value attributable to hazardous substances is generally measurable using the same methods and techniques that are used to measure depreciation from other causes. However, in some cases even environmental professionals cannot agree on the level of clean up required, the appropriate method of that clean up, or the cost.

The appraiser is cautioned that the value of a property impacted by environmental hazards may not be measurable simply by deducting the apparent costs or losses from the total value, as if "clean." The possibility of other changes affecting value, such as a change in highest and best use or even the marketability, should be considered.

S.R. 2-3, S.R. 5-3 and S.S.R. 1-2 require the appraiser to include, with each written report, a certification that states the name of each individual providing significant professional assistance. Accordingly, environmental engineers, inspectors and other professionals who prepare reports, furnish advice or make findings that are used in the appraisal process must be named on the certificate.

Under the Departure Provision, the appraiser may accept an assignment that would exclude the consideration of hazardous substances, provided that: the resulting appraisal is not misleading; the client has been advised of the limitation; and the report is qualified to reflect this limitation.

When there are no known hazardous substances it is recommended, as a matter of standard practice, for the appraiser to issue a disclaimer or limiting condition to the effect that the appraisal is predicated on the assumption that hazardous substances do not exist. No property can be assumed to be uncontaminated. If the property being appraised is not known[1] to be affected by hazardous substances and there is no reason to believe that it may be so affected, the issuance of such a disclaimer or limiting condition would not be considered to limit the scope of the appraisal. If the property being appraised is known to be affected by hazardous substances, or if there is reason to believe that it may be so affected, the appraiser cannot exclude the consideration of such materials without limiting the scope of the appraisal. In such appraisals, the appraiser must take great care to make sure that the limitation is not misleading.

If a property is known to be affected by hazardous substances, or if there is reason to believe that a property may be so affected, it may serve a valid and useful purpose to obtain an appraisal of the property, excluding the consideration of hazardous substances. Such an appraisal could be required as the logical starting point in a study of the impact of hazardous substances or in connection with legal proceedings. Whatever the purpose, such an appraisal must be properly qualified to prevent its misuse. The valuation of property, as if unaffected by hazards that are known to be present or are suspected of being present, would be predicated on an extraordinary assumption and therefore subject to S.R. 2-1(c) without exception. S.R. 2-1(c) requires that each written or oral real estate appraisal report must clearly and accurately disclose any extraordinary assumption or limiting condition that directly affects the appraisal and indicate its impact on value. S.R. 2-2(k) requires that the report clearly identify and explain any permitted departures from the regular requirements.

In limited assignments such as discussed above, the requirements of the Departure Provision, S.R. 2-1(c) and S.R.2-2(k) may be satisfied by including a suitable disclosure or limiting condition, an appropriate statement of purpose and properly qualified conclusions in the report. For purposes of illustration, assume that a property known to contain friable asbestos is to be appraised in accordance with the client's instructions, as if unaffected by asbestos. The report for such an appraisal would require a limiting condition, an appropriate statement of purpose and qualified conclusions similar in content to the following example.

> In accordance with the client's instructions, the estimated value reported herein reflects the total value of the subject property, as if unaffected by asbestos. It is reported that asbestos is present within the subject property. The presence of asbestos may have a negative influence on the value of the subject property, but the consideration of the effects of asbestos on the value of the subject property is beyond the purpose and scope of this appraisal. The appraiser cautions against the use of this appraisal without knowledge of the intended purpose and limited scope of the appraisal.

1. Knowledge is being defined here to mean obvious to the untrained person or specifically communicated through a reasonably reliable source.

In addition to an appropriate limiting condition such as shown above, there should be an appropriate statement of purpose and the conclusion should be properly qualified, as illustrated below.

The purpose of this appraisal is to estimate the market value of the subject property, as if unaffected by asbestos, as of January 1, 19XX.

The appraiser's final opinion of the market value of the subject property, as if unaffected by asbestos, as of January 1, 19XX is therefore $XX,XXX,XXX.

The limiting condition(s) should be stated in the letter of transmittal, if any, the body of the report, and whenever the report conclusion is stated.

Standard Disclaimers and Statements of Limiting Conditions

As previously mentioned, it is recommended practice, even in the appraisal of property where there is no reason to believe that the property is affected by hazardous substances, to include a standard disclaimer or statement of limiting conditions that pertains specifically to hazardous substances in the appraisal report. Such statements are not required by the Standards of Professional Practice, and they are not intended to limit the scope of the appraisal to something less than would otherwise be required. Rather, they are intended to clarify the normal limits of the appraisal, disclose the appraiser's lack of expertise with respect to hazardous substances, and disclaim the appraiser's responsibility for matters beyond the appraiser's level of expertise.

The following example is offered for illustration only.

Unless otherwise stated in this report, the existence of hazardous substances, including without limitation asbestos, polychlorinated biphenyls, petroleum leakage, or agricultural chemicals, which may or may not be present on the property, or other environmental conditions, were not called to the attention of nor did the appraiser become aware of such during the appraiser's inspection. The appraiser has no knowledge of the existence of such materials on or in the property unless otherwise stated. The appraiser, however, is not qualified to test such substances or conditions. If the presence of such substances, such as asbestos, urea formaldehyde foam insulation, or other hazardous substances or environmental conditions, may affect the value of the property, the value estimated is predicated on the assumption that there is no such condition on or in the property or in such proximity thereto that it would cause a loss in value. No responsibility is assumed for any such conditions, nor for any expertise or engineering knowledge required to discover them.

There is no suggestion that the preceding statement or any other disclaimer or limiting condition would be appropriate in all jurisdictions and circumstances. Appraisers are advised to consult their own legal counsel for assistance in developing individualized language for limiting conditions statements. Such statements may be considered in determining the extent of the appraiser's liability, if any, in connection with hazardous substances, and in determining whether the appraiser is eligible for errors and omissions liability insurance in connection with appraisals involving the consideration of hazardous substances.

The appraiser should note in the report any condition that is observed during the inspection of the subject property or becomes known to the appraiser through the normal research involved in performing the appraisal which would lead the appraiser to believe that hazardous substances may be present in or on the subject property, or is at variance with information or descriptions provided by others.

Unacceptable Practices

In the appraisal of property that requires the consideration of hazardous substances, but where the appraiser does not have the knowledge or experience required to detect the presence of such hazards or to measure the quantities of such hazards, the following practices are unacceptable.

1. Failure to disclose to the client the appraiser's lack of knowledge and experience with respect to the detection and measurement of hazardous substances (See Competency Provision).

2. Failure to take the necessary steps to complete the assignment competently such as personal study by the appraiser, association with another appraiser who has the required knowledge and experience or obtaining the professional assistance of others who possess the required knowledge and experience (See Competency Provision).

In the appraisal of property that is affected by hazardous substances, but where the purpose of the appraisal is to estimate value as if unaffected by hazardous substances, the following practice is unacceptable.

3. Failure to include in the report a qualification that reflects the limited scope of the appraisal, a limiting condition that clearly reveals the fact that the property is appraised as if unaffected by hazardous substances, an appropriate statement of purpose and properly qualified conclusions (See Departure Provision, S.R. 2-1(c) and S.R. 2-2(k)).

4. Failure to report known hazardous substances affecting the property (See S.R. 2-1(b) and S.R. 2-2(c)).

In the appraisal of property affected by hazardous substances, if the appraiser relies upon the findings of other professionals with respect to the presence of, and the probable effects of, hazardous substances, the following practice is unacceptable.

5. Failure to acknowledge the professional assistance of others and to name the persons providing the assistance in the certificate (See S.R. 2-3, S.R. 5-3 and S.S.R. 1-2).

(Please Note: Guide Notes to the Standards of Professional Appraisal Practice are an integral part of the Standards document. Guide Notes illustrate how the requirements of the Standards should be applied in various situations. Guide Notes should not be considered without referring to the Standards of Professional Practice.)

Subject   Retrospective Value Estimates

The Issue   Two dates are essential to an appraisal report. Standards Rule 2-2(e) requires that each appraisal report specify the effective date of the appraisal and the date of the report. The date of the report indicates the perspective from which the appraiser is examining the market. The effective date of the appraisal establishes the context for the value estimate. Three categories of effective dates—retrospective, current, or prospective—may be used according to the purpose and function of the appraisal assignment. When a retrospective effective date is used, how can the appraisal be prepared and presented in a manner that is not misleading?

The Statement   Retrospective appraisals (effective date of the appraisal prior to the date of the report) may be required for property tax matters, estate or inheritance tax matters, condemnation proceedings, suits to recover damages, and similar situations.

Current appraisals occur when the effective date of the appraisal is contemporaneous with the date of the report. Since most appraisals require current value estimates, the importance of specifying both the date of the report and effective date of the analysis is sometimes lost.

Prospective appraisals (effective date of the appraisal subsequent to the date of the report) may be required for valuations of property interest related to proposed developments, as the basis for value at the end of a cash flow projection, and for other reasons. (See SMT-4 on Prospective Value Estimates.)

The use of clear and concise language and appropriate terminology in appraisal reports helps to eliminate the preparation of misleading reports. To avoid confusion, the appraiser must clearly establish the date to which the value estimate applies. In retrospective value estimates, use of a modifier for the term market value and past verb tenses increases clarity (e.g. "...the retrospective market value was..." instead of "...the market value is...").

A retrospective appraisal is complicated by the fact that the appraiser already knows what occurred in the market after the effective date of the appraisal. Data subsequent to the effective date may be considered in estimating a retrospective value as a confirmation of trends that would reasonably be considered by a buyer or seller as of that date. The appraiser should determine a logical cut-off since, at some point distant from the effective date, the subsequent data will not reflect the relevant market. This is a difficult determination to make. Studying the market conditions as of the date of the appraisal assists the appraiser in judging where he or she should make this cut-off. In the absence of evidence in the market that data subsequent to the effective date was consistent with and confirmed market expectations as of the effective date, the effective date should be used as the cut-off date for data considered by the appraiser.

Use of direct excerpts from then current appraisal reports prepared at the time of the retrospective effective date helps the appraiser and the reader understand market conditions as of the retrospective effective date.

Adopted unanimously on July 8, 1991.

Appraisal Standards Board

John J. Leary, Chairman
Sherwood Darington, Vice Chairman
Charles B. Akerson
Daniel A. Dinote, Jr.
John L. Gadd

Subject   Prospective Value Estimates

The Issue   Two dates are essential to an appraisal report. Standards Rule 2-2(e) requires that each appraisal report specify the effective date of the appraisal and the date of the report. The date of the report indicates the perspective from which the appraiser is examining the market. The effective date of the appraisal establishes the context for the value estimate. Three categories of effective dates—retrospective, current, or prospective—may be used according to the purpose and function of the appraisal assignment. When a prospective effective date is used, how can the appraisal be prepared and presented in a manner that is not misleading?

The Statement   Retrospective appraisals (effective date of the appraisal prior to the date of the report) may be required for property tax matters, estate or inheritance tax matters, condemnation proceedings, suits to recover damages, and similar situations. (See SMT-3 on Retrospective Value Estimates.)

Current appraisals occur when the effective date of the appraisal is contemporaneous with the date of the report. Since most appraisals require current value estimates, the importance of specifying both the date of the report and effective date of the analysis is sometimes lost.

Prospective appraisals (effective date of the appraisal subsequent to the date of the report) may be required for valuations of property interest related to proposed developments, as the basis for value at the end of a cash flow projection, and for other reasons.

The use of clear and concise language and appropriate terminology in appraisal reports helps to eliminate the preparation of misleading reports. To avoid confusion, the appraiser must clearly establish the date to which the value estimate applies. In prospective value estimates, use of the term market value without a modifier such as forecasted or prospective and without future verb tenses is improper (i.e., "...the prospective market value is expected to be..." and not "...the market value is...").

Prospective value estimates are intended to reflect the current expectations and perceptions of market participants along with available factual data. They should be judged on the market support for the forecasts when made, not whether specific items in the forecasts are realized.

When prospective value estimates are required with regard to proposed improvements, Standards Rule 1-4(h) regarding the scope, character and probable time of completion of the proposed improvements and Standards Rule 1-4(c) regarding the basis for anticipated future rent and expenses are relevant. Evidence that proposed improvements can be completed by the effective date of the appraisal is important. Support for estimated income and expenses at the time of completion of proposed improvements and during the rent-up or sell-our period requires the incorporation of sufficient market research in the appraisal and the consideration of existing and future competition. It is appropriate to study comparable projects for evidence of construction periods, development costs, income and expense levels, and absorption. Items such as rental concessions, commissions, tenant finish allowances, add-on factors, and expense pass-throughs, must be studied to estimate realistic income expectancy.

With regard to proposed developments, two prospective value estimates may be required: as of the time the development is to be completed and as of the time the development is projected to achieve stabilized occupancy. These prospective values form a basis for investment decisions and loan underwriting.

In a prospective appraisal, the appraiser analyzes market trends to provide support for forecasted income and expense or sell-out estimates, absorption periods, capitalization rates, and discount rates as of the effective date of the appraisal. Economic trends such as growth in population, employment, and future competition are also analyzed. The overall economic climate and variations in the business cycle should be considered and weighed in the performance of the valuation process. All value conclusions should include reference to the time frame when the analysis was prepared to clearly delineate the market conditions and point of reference from which the appraiser developed the prospective value estimate. It is essential to include a limiting condition citing the market conditions from which the prospective value estimate was made and indicating that the appraiser cannot be held responsible for unforeseeable events that alter market conditions prior to the effective date of the appraisal.

Adopted unanimously on July 8, 1991.

Appraisal Standards Board

John J. Leary, Chairman
Sherwood Darington, Vice Chairman
Charles B. Akerson
Daniel A. Dinote, Jr.
John L. Gadd

Subject   Confidentiality Rule of the ETHICS PROVISION
The Confidentiality rule and the explanatory comment relating to this rule are stated below:

An appraiser must protect the confidential nature of the appraiser-client relationship.

Comment: An appraiser must not disclose confidential factual data obtained from a client or the results of an assignment prepared for a client to anyone other than: 1) the client and persons specifically authorized by the client; 2) such third parties as may be authorized by due process of law; and 3) a duly authorized professional peer review committee. As a corollary, it is unethical for a member of a duly authorized professional peer review committee to disclose confidential information or factual data presented to the committee.

The Issue   The appraiser-client relationship begins with and is governed by a written or oral contract of engagement between the appraiser and the client. What are the confidential aspects of the appraiser-client relationship that the appraiser must protect under the USPAP?

The Statement   Fiduciary responsibilities are inherent in professional appraisal practice. The confidential nature of the appraiser's relationship with the client was recognized by the appraisal profession before December 4, 1989, the date of the ETHICS PROVISION amendment to the USPAP, as evidenced by codes of professional ethics of a number of professional appraisal organizations.

The obligation of the appraiser to protect the confidential nature of the appraiser-client relationship is neither absolute nor clearly understood.

Under USPAP, an appraiser must act in good faith with regard to the legitimate interests of the client in the use of the written or oral appraisal report and the disclosure of confidential elements of the appraisal report or disclosure of confidential information given to the appraiser by the client for use in connection with the appraisal.

Obviously, there is no violation of the Confidentiality rule when an appraiser discloses the results of an assignment or confidential factual data obtained from a client to the client and all other persons specifically authorized by the client.

However, the appraiser-client relationship envisioned in the USPAP is not comparable, for example, to the attorney-client relationship because there is no violation of the Confidentiality rule when an appraiser discloses, without the client's permission, the results of an assignment or confidential factual data obtained from a client to third parties authorized under due process of law or to a duly authorized professional peer review committee. Disclosure under these circumstances serves the superior interests of the public and the appraisal profession in uncovering suppression of material information or advocacy through misuse or abuse of the Confidentiality rule.

The results of an assignment prepared for a client are the appraiser's analyses, opinions, and conclusions pertinent to the assignment. These are clearly confidential matters under the USPAP and may only be disclosed to the three groups cited in the comment to the Confidentiality rule.

Under the USPAP, an appraiser may only disclose confidential data obtained from client to the persons within the same three cited groups. Consequently, the meaning of "confidential factual data obtained from the client" is critically important because factual data obtained from a client that is not deemed confidential may be disclosed by an appraiser without the client's permission.

Market data is necessary to the appraisal profession and the quality of work that the public has a right to expect from professionals. To hold that all factual data obtained from the client are confidential simply because they were given to the appraiser for use in connection with the appraisal is an extremely broad and arbitrary construction that unduly burdens the appraiser without a compensating benefit to the public. Less available data tends to diminish the quality of appraisal services.

With regard to factual data supplied to the appraiser by the client, the client is in the best position to decide what data must be considered confidential and to provide an explanation for such a determination. The USPAP recognize that such data are to be treated as confidential only when the client specifically instructs the appraiser that the factual data are confidential .. Data furnished by the client to potential buyers or mortgagees without a confidentiality condition do not become confidential when given to the appraiser. All other factual data obtained by the appraiser from any source are not recognized as confidential by the USPAP, unless the appraiser knows of the confidential nature of the data.

When the appraisal report is addressed to the client, any confidential factual data given to the appraiser by the client and relied upon in the appraiser's analyses, opinions, or conclusions may be specifically cited in the report without violation of the Confidentiality rule.

Adopted unanimously on September 10, 1991.

Appraisal Standards Board

John J. Leary, Chairman
Sherwood Darington, Vice Chairman
Charles B. Akerson
Daniel A. Dinote, Jr.
John L. Gadd

Statement on Appraisal Standards No. 6 (SMT-6)

Statements on Appraisal Standards are authorized by the by-laws of The Appraisal Foundation and are specifically for the purpose of clarification, interpretation, explanation or elaboration of the Uniform Standards of Professional Appraisal Practice (USPAP). Statements have the full weight of a standards rule and can only be adopted by the Appraisal Standards Board (ASB) after exposure and comment.

Subject

Reasonable Exposure Time in Market Value Estimates

The Issue

In the USPAP, the Comment to Standards Rule 1-2 (b) states:

When estimating market value, the appraiser should be specific as to the estimate of exposure time linked to the value estimate.

The Comment to Standards Rule 2-2 (e) states:

...Defining the value to be estimated requires both an appropriately referenced definition and any comments needed to clearly indicate to the reader how the definition is being applied [See Standards Rule 1-2 (b)].

How is this reasonable exposure time estimated? When is it presumed to occur, i.e., prior to or starting from the effective date of the appraisal?

The Statement

Reasonable exposure time is one of a series of conditions in most market value definitions. Exposure time is always presumed to precede the effective date of the appraisal.

Exposure time may be defined as follows: The estimated length of time the property interest being appraised would have been offered on the market prior to the hypothetical consummation of a sale at market value on the effective date of the appraisal; a retrospective estimate based upon an analysis of past events assuming a competitive and open market.

Exposure time is different for various types of real estate and under various market conditions. It is noted that the overall concept of reasonable exposure encompasses not only adequate, sufficient and reasonable time but also adequate, sufficient and reasonable effort. This statement focuses on the time component.

The fact that exposure time is always presumed to occur prior to the effective date of the appraisal is substantiated by related facts in the appraisal process: supply/demand conditions as of the effective date of the appraisal; the use of current cost information; the analysis of historical sales information (sold after exposure and after completion of negotiations between the seller and buyer); and the analysis of future income expectancy estimated from the effective date of the appraisal.

Rationale and Method for Estimating Reasonable Exposure Time

The estimate of the time period for reasonable exposure is not intended to be a prediction of a date of sale or a one-line statement. Instead, it is an integral part of the analyses conducted during the appraisal assignment. The estimate may be expressed as a range and can be based on one or more of the following:

- statistical information about days on market;
- information gathered through sales verification; and,
- interviews of market participants.

Related information garnered through this process include the identification of typical buyers and sellers for the type of real estate involved and typical equity investment levels and/or financing terms.

The reasonable exposure period is a function of price, time and use, not an isolated estimate of time alone. As an example, an office building could have been on the market for two years at a price of $2,000,000 that informed market participants considered unreasonable. Then, the owner lowers the price to $1,600,000 and starts to receive offers, culminating in a transaction at $1,400,000 six months later. While the actual exposure time was 2.5 years, the reasonable exposure time at a value range of $1,400,000 to $1,600,000 would be six months. The answer to the question "what is reasonable exposure time?" should always incorporate the answers to the question "for what kind of real estate at what value range?" rather than appear as a statement of an isolated time period.

Discussion of Exposure Time in the Appraisal Report

The discussion of reasonable exposure time should appear in an appropriate section of the appraisal report that presents the discussion and analysis of market conditions and be referenced at the statement of the value definition and value conclusion.

Applications to Client Uses of an Appraisal

When an appraisal is commissioned as the result of a mortgage application after a potential seller and buyer enter into a Contract for Sale, no conflict exists between the presumption in the appraisal process that exposure time occurs prior to the effective date of the appraisal and the function (client use) of the appraisal.

When an appraisal is commissioned for employee relocation, asset evaluation, foreclosure, or asset management purposes, the presumption in the appraisal process that exposure time occurs prior to the effective date of the appraisal may conflict with the function of the appraisal as envisioned by the client.

Problems arise when clients attempt to make business decisions or account for assets without understanding the difference between reasonable exposure time and marketing time (see related Advisory Opinion G-7 on Marketing Time Estimates).

Conclusions
— The reasonable exposure time inherent in the market value concept is always presumed to precede the effective date of the appraisal.

— Exposure time is different for various types of real estate and under various market conditions.

— The answers to the question "what is reasonable exposure time?" should always incorporate the answer to the question "for what kind of real estate at what value range?" rather than appear as a statement of an isolated time period.

Adopted unanimously on September 16, 1992.

Appraisal Standards Board

John J. Leary, Chairman
Sherwood Darington, Vice Chairman
Daniel A. Dinote, Jr.
John L. Gadd
Ritch LeGrand

Advisory Opinion G-1

This communication by the Appraisal Standards Board (ASB) does not establish new standards or interpret existing standards. Advisory Opinions are issued to illustrate the applicability of appraisal standards in specific situations and to offer advice from the ASB for the resolution of appraisal issues and problems.

Subject	Sales History

The Issue

The Uniform Standards of Professional Appraisal Practice (USPAP) and supplemental standards issued by others contain sales history provisions which require appraisers of real property to consider, analyze and report pending and recent agreements, options, listings and sales involving the property being appraised. Because of differences in state laws and operating practices relating to the disclosure and confidentiality of real property sales data, the ways in which appraisers comply with the sales history provisions vary according to the jurisdiction and the availability of information. This lack of consistency has raised questions regarding the applicability and relevance of the sales history provisions.

How can the appraiser best comply with the sales history provisions of the applicable appraisal standards in the face of obstacles that are beyond the control of the appraiser?

Advice from the ASB on the Issue

This Advisory Opinion offers advice and guidance for compliance with the requirements to consider, analyze and report sales history and related information in the appraisal of real property.

USPAP Standards Rule 1-5(a, b) requires an appraiser to consider and analyze (a) any current Agreement of Sale, option, or listing of the property being appraised, if such information is available to the appraiser in the normal course of business and (b) any prior sales of the property being appraised that occurred within one year for a one- to four-family residential property or three years for all other property types. In any case, USPAP Standards Rule 2-2(k) calls for the written appraisal report to contain sufficient information to indicate compliance with the sales history provision. Standards Rule 2-2(k) further requires that, if sales history information is unobtainable, the written appraisal report must include a commentary on the efforts taken by the appraiser to obtain the information.

Supplemental Standards issued by regulatory agencies and eminent domain authorities also contain provisions which require the appraiser to analyze and report sales history information, and these requirements vary according to jurisdiction.

The requirement for the appraiser to consider, analyze and report sales history and related information is fundamental to the appraisal process. Just as the appraiser must take into account pending and recent sales of comparable property, the appraiser must take into account any pending and recent sales of the subject property itself.

This is not to say that the agreed price in a pending or recent sale of the subject property is necessarily representative of value as defined in the report, but the appraiser's failure to consider, analyze and report these facts may exclude important information from the sales comparison approach to value. Information pertaining to the current market status and the sales history of the subject property may also be useful information for the determination of highest and best use or the analysis of market trends.

Sample Sales Histories

The following sample sales histories are offered as examples of information that might be included in an appraisal report in compliance with the applicable standards. The sales data is fictitious and is shown only for purposes of illustration.

For a commercial property that is not under agreement or option, is not offered for sale on the open market and has not changed hands within the past three years, the sales history might be shown in the appraisal report as follows:

> The owner reports that the subject property is not under current agreement or option and is not offered for sale on the open market. According to public records, the subject property has not changed hands during the past three years.

For a commercial property that is offered for sale on the open market and was acquired by the current owner during the past year, the sales history to be included in the appraisal report might appear as follows:

> The subject property is currently offered for sale at a listing price of $XXX,XXX. A copy of the listing agreement with Mary Smith, real estate broker, is included in the addendum to this report.

> The subject property was sold by John Jones to the current owner on June 1, 19XX for a reported price of $XXX,XXX. The parties to the transaction have affirmed that the seller received all cash and that the reported price was unaffected by special or creative financing or sales concessions granted by anyone associated with the sale. This sale is analyzed in the Sales Comparison Approach section of the appraisal report.

> According to the public records, there have been no other transfers of the subject property within the past year.

Sample Comments

The following sample comments are offered as examples of comments that might be included in an appraisal report in cases where pertinent information is not available to the appraiser in the normal course of business. The comments are fictitious and are offered only for purposes of illustration.

In cases where the property being appraised is known to be the subject of a pending transaction, but where the appraiser is not privy to the terms of the pending transaction, and where the parties to the transaction have declined to disclose the terms of the transactions to the appraiser, the sales history to be included in the appraisal report might include a comment such as the one shown below:

> The property being appraised is known to be the subject of a pending purchase and sale agreement, but the appraiser was unable to obtain the terms of the agreement. The current owner confirmed that the property is under agreement, but declined to disclose the terms of the agreement or to discuss the nature of the agreement.

In jurisdictions where reliable price information cannot be found in the public records, and where the appraiser is unable to obtain complete information in the normal course of business, it would be appropriate to include in the appraisal report a comment similar to the one shown below:

> The subject property was sold by John Jones to the current owner on June 1, 19XX for an unknown price. The appraiser attempted to obtain the purchase price and other terms of the transaction without success. The parties to the transaction declined to discuss the terms or conditions of the sale.

According to the public records, there have been no other transfers of the subject property within the past three years.

This Advisory Opinion is based on presumed conditions without investigation or verification of actual circumstances. There is no assurance that this Advisory Opinion represents the only possible solution to the problems discussed or that it applies equally to seemingly similar situations.

Adopted unanimously on December 3, 1990.

Appraisal Standards Board

John J. Leary, Chairman
Sherwood Darington, Vice Chairman
Charles B. Akerson
Daniel A. Dinote, Jr.
John L. Gadd

Advisory Opinion G-2

This communication by the Appraisal Standards Board (ASB) does not establish new standards or interpret existing standards. Advisory Opinions are issued to illustrate the applicability of appraisal standards in specific situations and to offer advice from the ASB for the resolution of appraisal issues and problems.

Subject	Inspection of Subject Property Real Estate

The Issue	What constitutes a minimum inspection of the real estate of the subject property under the applicable standards of the Uniform Standards of Professional Appraisal Practice (USPAP)? Under what conditions is a "drive-by" appraisal permissible?

Advice from the ASB on the Issue

The elements of USPAP relating to inspection of real estate for the purpose of developing an appraisal require that the appraiser adequately identify the real estate, consider the purpose and intended use of the appraisal, consider the extent of the data collection process, identify any special limiting conditions, and identify the effective date of the appraisal. USPAP also mandates that each written appraisal report must contain a signed certification that requires each individual signing the appraisal report to certify that he or she has or has not made a personal inspection of the property. The extent and depth of the inspection process varies with the type of property appraised and the conditions of the appraisal. This Advisory Opinion addresses only the minimum general requirements of the inspection process, with no discussion of special requirements or property types.

It is the appraiser's responsibility to determine if adequate information is available about the subject real estate to develop a real property appraisal that conforms with the USPAP. An appraiser cannot rationally develop an appraisal if adequate information on the subject real estate is not available. Consequently, where physical characteristics information is not available through an opportunity for a complete inspection or from reliable third party sources, an appraiser has the duty to obtain the necessary information to develop the appraisal before continuing or to withdraw from the assignment.

Many appraisals involve an inspection of the land and an exterior and interior inspection of the existing improvements by an appraiser on a "walk-through" basis. This type of inspection is not necessarily the equivalent of an inspection by a qualified engineer. An appraiser's inspection should, at the minimum, be thorough enough to (a) adequately describe the real estate in the appraisal report, (b) develop an opinion of highest and best use, when such an opinion is necessary and appropriate, and (c) make meaningful comparisons in the valuation of the property.

There are situations where interior and complete exterior inspections are not possible as of the effective date of the appraisal. For example, inspections are not physically possible where improvements have been destroyed, removed, or not yet built. Inspections are not legally or contractually possible if the appraiser is denied access by the property owner or if the contract stipulates a "drive-by" appraisal.

Where an interior and complete exterior inspection is not possible for any valid reasons, physical characteristics information about the real estate should be obtained from reliable third party sources in the form of photographs, public information from local assessors and other governmental agencies, and private information from multiple listing and other data service firms and files of individuals. The same sources that are utilized to research and verify comparable sales data can be used to obtain information about the subject property. An appraisal developed without the benefit of an interior and complete exterior inspection by the appraiser is subject to the same standards that would apply if the appraiser had made a complete personal inspection.

An appraisal report with a certification stating a personal inspection was made represents that the performed inspection was sufficient to satisfy all the requirements of the applicable standards rules. If a personal inspection was made of a property with existing enclosed improvements and the inspection was limited to an external observation, this limitation should be disclosed. On the other hand, an inspection of a property consisting of land only without enclosed improvement would require no such disclosure.

An appraisal report may contain a certification stating that a personal inspection was not made by the appraiser. Simply disclosing this fact, however, does not relieve the appraiser of the responsibility to determine whether adequate information about the subject real estate is available to develop an appraisal that is not meaningless or misleading.[1]

Examples of Special Limiting Conditions

The examples cited below are illustrations of the wording of a special limiting condition in an appraisal report for a client that requested a drive-by appraisal.

> The appraiser has been requested to perform a drive-by appraisal and not to disturb the occupants by entering the building. The physical characteristics used to develop this appraisal are based on an inspection that the appraiser made three years ago when the property was appraised for estate tax purposes. For the purpose of this appraisal it is assumed that the interior condition of the subject property has not materially changed during the past three years. The subject property was observed from the public street as of the effective date of the appraisal. This exterior inspection revealed that the outside of the building has been repainted and the roof has been replaced.

or

> The appraiser has been requested to perform a drive-by appraisal and not to disturb the occupants by entering the building. The physical characteristics used to develop this appraisal are based on the assessment records of (cite jurisdiction) and on the multiple

---

1. See Advisory Opinion G-5.

listing service information of (cite source). The subject property was observed from the public street as of the effective date of the appraisal. Based on the observed conditions the assessment records and multiple listing service information appear to be accurate. For the purposes of this appraisal it is assumed that the interior condition of the subject property is consistent with the exterior conditions as observed and that the information concerning the interior condition as provided by the assessor's records and the multiple listing service is accurate.

This Advisory Opinion is based on presumed conditions without investigation or verification of actual circumstances. There is no assurance that this Advisory Opinion represents the only possible solution to the problems discussed or that it applies equally to seemingly similar situations.

Approved for general distribution on December 4, 1990.

Appraisal Standards Board

John J. Leary, Chairman
Sherwood Darington, Vice Chairman
Charles B. Akerson
Daniel A. Dinote, Jr.
John L. Gadd

Advisory Opinion G-4

This communication by the Appraisal Standards Board (ASB) does not establish new standards or interpret existing standards. Advisory Opinions are issued to illustrate the applicability of appraisal standards in specific situations and to offer advice from the ASB for the resolution of appraisal issues and problems.

Subject	STANDARDS RULE 1-5(b)

The Issue

Standards Rule 1-5(b) requires an appraiser to consider and analyze any prior sales of the property being appraised that occurred within one year for one- to four-family residential property and three years for all other property types. Must a transfer of title in lieu of foreclosure or a foreclosure sale be considered and analyzed?

Advice from the ASB on the Issue

The intent of Standards Rule 1-5(b) is to encourage the research and analysis of prior sales of the subject property. Any prior sales of the appraised property within the prescribed period stated in Standards Rule 1-5(b) includes transfers in lieu of foreclosure and foreclosure sales.

A voluntary transfer of title by mortgagor to mortgagee in lieu of foreclosure as well as a foreclosure sale are grounded in objective necessity. Nevertheless, they are sales because they transfer ownership of and title to property for a valuable consideration. With research and analysis, an appraiser is able to report under Standards Rule 2-2(k) that a prior sale of the subject property is influenced by undue stimulation or the sale does not reflect buyer and seller typical motivation.

This Advisory Opinion is based on presumed conditions without investigation or verification of actual circumstances. There is no assurance that this Advisory Opinion represents the only possible solution to the problems discussed or that it applies equally to seemingly similar situations.

Approved for general distribution on June 3, 1991.

Appraisal Standards Board

John J. Leary, Chairman
Sherwood Darington, Vice Chairman
Charles B. Akerson
Daniel A. Dinote, Jr.
John L. Gadd

Advisory Opinion G-7

This communication by the Appraisal Standards Board (ASB) does not establish new standards or interpret existing standards. Advisory Opinions are issued to illustrate the applicability of appraisal standards in specific situations and to offer advice from the ASB for the resolution of appraisal issues and problems.

Subject   Marketing Time Estimates

The Issue   The Uniform Standards of Professional Appraisal Practice recognize that supplemental standards applicable to appraisals prepared for specific purposes or property types may be issued by public agencies and certain client groups. Some of these supplemental standards require the appraiser to analyze and report a reasonable marketing period for the subject property when estimating the market value of real property.

How is this reasonable marketing period estimated and what is the relationship of this estimate of marketing time to the appraisal process?

Advice from the ASB on the Issue   The reasonable marketing time is an estimate of the amount of time it might take to sell a property interest in real estate at the estimated market value level during the period immediately after the effective date of an appraisal.

Marketing time differs from exposure time, which is always presumed to precede the effective date of an appraisal. (See Statement on Appraisal Standards No. 6 on <u>Reasonable Exposure Time in Market Value Estimates.</u>)

Rationale and Method for Estimating Marketing Time   The estimate of marketing time uses some of the same data analyzed in the process of estimating reasonable exposure time as part of the appraisal process and is not intended to be a prediction of a date of sale or a one-line statement. It is an integral part of the analyses conducted during the appraisal assignment. The estimate may be expressed as a range and can be based on one or more of the following:

- statistical information about days on market;
- information gathered through sales verification;
- interviews of market participants; and
- anticipated changes in market conditions.

Related information garnered through this process include other market conditions that may affect marketing time, such as the identification of typical buyers and sellers for the type of real estate involved and typical equity investment levels and/or financing terms. The reasonable marketing time is a function of price, time, use, and anticipated market conditions such as changes in the cost and availability of funds, not an isolated estimate of time alone.

Discussion of Marketing Time in the Appraisal Report

Since marketing time occurs after the effective date of the market value estimate and the marketing time estimate is related to, yet apart from the appraisal process, it is appropriate for the section of the appraisal report that discusses this issue and its implications to appear toward the end of the report after the market value conclusion. The request to estimate a reasonable marketing time exceeds the normal information required for the conduct of the appraisal process, and should be treated separately from that process.

It is also appropriate for the appraiser to discuss the impact of price/value relationships on marketing time and contrast different potential prices and the associated marketing time with the reasonable marketing time at the estimate of market value.

Applications to Client Uses of an Appraisal

Clients concerned with marketing real estate that obtain a market value appraisal as part of their decision-making process should be aware that it may be inappropriate to assume that the value remains stable during the marketing period. Therefore, it is technically incorrect for the user of an appraisal to take a current value estimate, carry it forward to the end of an estimated marketing period, and then discount back to the present.

Some clients attempt to solve their problem by ordering a "120-day market value," a "six-month market value," or a "one-year market value" from the appraiser. Unless the estimate of reasonable exposure time made by the appraiser in the course of such an assignment coincides with the pre-condition imposed by the client, the answer to this assignment cannot be stated as market value under a typical definition of the term. In such situations, the appraiser must clearly distinguish between a market value estimate allowing for reasonable exposure time and any alternative, appropriately defined value estimates subject to a special limiting condition citing the client-imposed marketing time.

Whether or not the appraiser and client define the appraisal problem to include more that one estimate of market value, the roles of the parties must be kept clear. The appraiser provides the client with a supported estimate of defined value in an appropriately documented report that includes a section on reasonable marketing time and any inherent price/value implications. The ultimate decision on issues like what price to ask, when to accept a particular offering price, and how to account for the asset during the interim rests with the client.

This Advisory Opinion is based on presumed conditions without investigation or verification of actual circumstances. There is no assurance that this Advisory Opinion represents the only possible solution to the problems discussed or that it applies equally to seemingly similar situations.

Approved for general distribution on September 16, 1992.

Appraisal Standards Board

John J. Leary, Chairman
Sherwood Darington, Vice Chairman
Daniel A. Dinote, Jr.
John L. Gadd
Ritch LeGrand

Standards Rule 2-1   Each written or oral real property appraisal report must:

(a) clearly and accurately set forth the appraisal in a manner that will not be misleading;

(b) contain sufficient information to enable the person(s) who receive or rely on the report to understand it properly;

(c) clearly and accurately disclose any extraordinary assumption or limiting condition that directly affects the appraisal and indicate its impact on value.

Standards Rule 2-2   Each written real property appraisal report must:

(a) identify and describe the real estate being appraised[1];

(b) identify the real property interest being appraised;

(c) state the purpose of the appraisal;

(d) define the value to be estimated;

(e) set forth the effective date of the appraisal and the date of the report[2];

(f) describe the extent of the process of collecting, confirming, and reporting data;

(g) set forth all assumptions and limiting conditions that affect the analyses, opinions, and conclusions;

(h) set forth the information considered, the appraisal procedures followed, and the reasoning that supports the analyses, opinions, and conclusions;

(i) set forth the appraiser's opinion of the highest and best use of the real estate, when such an opinion is necessary and appropriate;

(j) explain and support the exclusion of any of the usual valuation approaches;

(k) set forth any additional information that may be appropriate to show compliance with, or clearly identify and explain permitted departures from, the requirements of Standard 1;

(l) include a signed certification in accordance with Standards Rule 2-3.

---

1. See Advisory Opinion G-2.
2. See Statements on Appraisal Standards No. 3 and No. 4.

Standards Rule 2-3   Each written real property appraisal report must contain a certification that is similar in content to the following form:

I certify that, to the best of my knowledge and belief:

— the statements of fact contained in this report are true and correct.

— the reported analyses, opinions, and conclusions are limited only by the reported assumptions and limiting conditions, and are my personal, unbiased professional analyses, opinions, and conclusions.

— I have no (or the specified) present or prospective interest in the property that is the subject of this report, and I have no (or the specified) personal interest or bias with respect to the parties involved.

— my compensation is not contingent upon the reporting of a predetermined value or direction in value that favors the cause of the client, the amount of the value estimate, the attainment of a stipulated result, or the occurrence of a subsequent event.

— my analyses, opinions, and conclusions were developed, and this report has been prepared, in conformity with the Uniform Standards of Professional Appraisal Practice.

— I have (or have not) made a personal inspection of the property that is the subject of this report. (If more than one person signs the report, this certification must clearly specify which individuals did and which individuals did not make a personal inspection of the appraised property.)[1]

— no one provided significant professional assistance to the person signing this report. (If there are exceptions, the name of each individual providing significant professional assistance must be stated.)

1. See Advisory Opinions G-2 and G-5.

Standards Rule 2-5   An appraiser who signs a real property appraisal report prepared by another, even under the label of "review appraiser," must accept full responsibility for the contents of the report.[1]

1. See Advisory Opinion G-5.

133